Cultivating a Data
in Higher Educatio

CW00545367

Higher education institutions have experienced a sharp increase in demand for accountability. To meet the growing demand by legislators, accreditors, consumers, taxpayers, and parents for evidence of successful outcomes, this important book provides higher education leaders and practitioners with actionable strategies for developing a comprehensive data culture throughout the entire institution. Exploring key considerations necessary for the development of an effective data culture in colleges and universities, this volume brings together diverse voices and perspectives, including institutional researchers, senior academic leaders, and faculty. Each chapter focuses on a critical element of managing or influencing a data culture, approaches for breaking through common challenges, and concludes with practical, research-based implementation strategies. Collectively, these strategies form a comprehensive list of recommendations for developing a data culture and becoming a change agent within your higher education institution.

Kristina Powers is President of K Powers Consulting Inc. and Vice President of Institutional Effectiveness and Planning at Patten University, USA.

Angela E. Henderson is Director of Institutional Research and Effectiveness at Stetson University, USA.

Cultivating a Data Culture in Higher Education

Edited by Kristina Powers and Angela E. Henderson

Routledge
Taylor & Francis Group

NEW YORK AND LONDON

First published 2018
by Routledge
711 Third Avenue, New York, NY 10017

and by Routledge
2 Park Square, Milton Park, Abingdon, Oxon, OX14 4RN

Routledge is an imprint of the Taylor & Francis Group, an informa business

Library of Congress Cataloging-in-Publication Data
Names: Powers, Kristina, editor.
Title: Cultivating a data culture in higher education / [edited] by
Kristina Powers and Angela E. Henderson.
Description: New York, NY : Routledge, 2018. | Includes index.
Identifiers: LCCN 2018001659| ISBN 9781138046795 (hardback)
| ISBN 9781138046801 (pbk.) | ISBN 9781315171326 (ebook) |
ISBN 9781351694520
(Web PDF) | ISBN 9781351694513 (ePub) |
ISBN 9781351694506 (mobi/kindle)
Subjects: LCSH: Education, Higher–Data processing. | Educational
accountability.
Classification: LCC LB2395.7 .C84 2018 | DDC 378.0285–dc23
LC record available at https://lccn.loc.gov/2018001659

ISBN: 978-1-138-04679-5 (hbk)
ISBN: 978-1-138-04680-1 (pbk)
ISBN: 978-1-315-17132-6 (ebk)

Typeset in Perpetua
by Wearset Ltd, Boldon, Tyne and Wear

Dedication

To Tim Powers — for inspiring me to live life to its fullest and living it together.

Kristina Powers

Contents

CONTENTS

Figures

Tables

Preface

Using data in higher education institutions was nearly unheard of a century ago. Fast forward to 2018 with nearly every (if not all) higher education institution(s) experiencing widespread use of data in pursuit of effective decision-making. Among the biggest changes over the past decades has been the proliferation of data throughout the institution.

Data are being used, analyzed, synthesized, distributed, communicated, and interpreted by multiple offices and individuals within the institution. This diffusion of data served as the impetus for this book. With so many people and offices using data, this book aims to provide higher education leaders with ideas and practical suggestions for cultivating a data culture that complements the institution's existing culture.

Higher education has experienced a sharp increase in demand for data from external audiences such as legislators, accreditors, consumers, and taxpayers. This increased accountability, coupled with expectations of transparency and limited financial resources, has prompted post-secondary institutions to recognize the need for a comprehensive data culture throughout the entire institution. Despite this awareness, many institutions struggle with creating an effective and positive data culture due to the lack of experienced leadership to guide the process.

Absence of experience in leading a data culture is not surprising, given that higher education has spent the last sixty years focusing on data in the form of disparate analyses and reports. Little attention has been devoted to advancement of the skills and tools necessary for developing an institutional data culture, despite the proliferation of data usage across divisions and departments for at least a decade. As the scope and demand for data continue to expand, the ability to influence development of an intentional data culture is critical. This book is intended to provide higher education leaders and practitioners with practices and strategies for developing a holistic data culture.

Exploring key considerations necessary for the development of an effective data culture, this book brings together authors from different higher education experiences and perspectives, including institutional research, senior academic leaders, and faculty. Each chapter focuses on a critical element of managing or influencing a data culture and concludes with practical implementation strategies. The practical suggestions and guidance sections of each chapter provide specific approaches for breaking through common challenges in building a data culture, including a combination of practitioner-based experiences, best practices, and research-based evidence. These strategies provide readers with easy to implement recommendations for action related to specific chapter content. Collectively, these strategies form a comprehensive list of recommendations for developing a data culture within a higher education institution.

This book contains thirteen chapters organized within four key areas related to influencing a data culture: Part I: Importance, Planning, and Context; Part II: People, Leadership, and Relationships; Part III: Perceptions, Usability, and Communication; and Part IV: Putting the Culture Pieces Together.

Part I contains three chapters, emphasizing importance and context. Chapter 1 begins with fundamentals of defining and developing a data culture. At the core level, a data culture focuses on the use of information to make sound decisions that help an institution attain a competitive gain. Moving on, Chapter 2 offers specific strategies for higher education administrators in the early stage of planning to implement data analytics or in the middle of this challenging task. These practical strategies help practitioners avoid organizational obstacles and overcome cultural barriers while building an effective data culture. Chapter 3 spends time on the often-overlooked concept of data context. This chapter focuses on the importance of understanding the context of data and institutional environment to maximize change.

Part II examines an organization's most valuable asset—its people. This section delves further into the role that individuals play in developing a data culture through a focus on leadership and relationships in higher education institutions. This section begins with Chapter 4 and a focus on identifying decision makers to advance a data culture. Chapter authors present theoretical frameworks and practical factors to inform and support the cultural change needed for development of a data culture, such as ensuring trust, developing employees, and communicating success of data-based approaches.

Changing the data culture within higher education requires leaders to think differently. Chapter 5 focuses on the mind-shift leaders must undergo to help transform a data culture. Factors that influence perceptions of data are discussed in the context of the implicit and explicit assumptions they represent. Cognitive biases about data are examined and accompanied by practical activities to prompt a shift in mindset.

Furthering the discussion of leadership, Chapter 6 examines ways to foster data-informed leadership and overcome resistance to use of data for decision-making. Key strategic steps in leading a data culture are discussed in this chapter, as well as common barriers and misperceptions of data-informed leadership.

Chapter 7 moves the conversation forward by focusing on building relationships that benefit development of a data culture. This chapter emphasizes the importance of building relationships as a key strategy for developing a culture of evidence. Through a combination of shared vision, data-focused initiatives, professional expertise, and diverse thinking, institutions can cultivate and harness the power of critical thinking and analytical reasoning at the campus level. Individual experiences are highlighted throughout the chapter to illustrate the successes and challenges associated with a shift in institutional culture.

This section concludes with examination of a universal issue for administrators—managing the complexity and chaos inherent in transforming data into information. The combination of creating information and working with people results in a complex and often chaotic environment. If not managed properly, this environment can lead to wasted resources, duplication of work, faulty decisions, and overall dissatisfaction.

Part III focuses on the importance of user perceptions, practicality of data, and communication in the cultivation of a data culture. Chapter 9 explores disparity across data sources and helps readers determine appropriate data sources. This is especially critical when multiple sources for the same data exist within an institution, resulting in confusion and discrepancies. Awareness of how to determine the most appropriate source for data is critical to establishing a successful data culture. This chapter explores common data sources and provides insight into how to select the appropriate source for a given demand.

Building on the identification of appropriate data sources, the next step toward the development of a data culture is an intentional focus on making data practical and engaging. Content has traditionally been the focus of data reports, with minimal consideration given to form. Chapter 10 delves into the relationship between data and user experience; form influences perception and perception influences data use. It is in this sentiment that we find the key to creating usable data; the marriage of content and form that results in reports which encourage a culture of data use.

Chapter 11 addresses the common challenge of communicating and disseminating data in a way that ensures data are received by all decision makers with responsibilities relevant to the data, rather than a select few. This chapter focuses on factors affecting data communication such as awareness of audience, scope of data provided, and effective communication methods. Absence of a deliberate dissemination structure often results in an unhealthy (but perhaps merited) skepticism regarding data accessibility and hinders progress toward creating a data culture.

Part III closes with a topic that is typically not part of data discussions, but needs to be—risk. Chapter 12 provides a brief review of the history of risk management, including its theoretical inception and formalization, up to the very recent application of enterprise risk management (ERM) for colleges and universities. Some specific challenges faced by decision support leaders and professionals are discussed within the context of managing and mitigating risk.

Part IV distills the content of prior chapters to present a cohesive summary of information and strategies. Further, it provides an overview of how the topics addressed within the preceding chapters combine to create a foundation for an effective data culture within an institution.

It is the hope of the authors that this book will provide the foundation necessary for you to become a change agent in *Cultivating a Data Culture in Higher Education*.

Acknowledgments

We would like to express our heartfelt appreciation to those who have made this book possible. First, we would like to acknowledge all of the chapter authors who contributed their time and expertise. It is with great gratitude that we thank Routledge, especially our editor—Heather Jarrow. We are privileged to work with the dedicated and experienced team at Routledge.

We would like to thank the anonymous individuals who took the time to respond to Routledge's survey questionnaire, which guided us in the development of the book. We have incorporated much of the feedback and comments that consistently emerged; your early contributions resulted in an enhanced and robust publication.

Finally, an honorable mention goes to the family and friends of all contributors to this book; it is with their support that we are able to complete the research about which we are so passionate.

Part I

Importance, Planning, and Context

Chapter 1

Developing a Data Culture

Angela E. Henderson and Kristina Powers

WHAT IS A DATA CULTURE?

At the core level, a data culture focuses on the use of information to make sound decisions that help an institution attain a competitive gain. It is not a focus on numbers, but rather on effective use of resources to make advantageous decisions. Let us be clear that a data culture is not a reliance on figures at the expense of individuals with subject matter expertise within the institutions.

To some, the term "data" itself implies a dehumanizing stigma; however, effective data use relies entirely on the knowledge, context, and interpretation of institutional stakeholders. Data is not dehumanizing, but seeks to bring stakeholders together to a shared understanding and communication of institutional information. A data culture is not a culture of numbers or accountability, but rather one of awareness resulting from alignment and entwinement of institutional environment, individuals within the environment, and actions, contextualized through the lens of data (Figure 1.1). In this environment, through cultivation and involvement, data becomes information.

With increasing federal, state, and external reporting expectations, data has become synonymous with accountability in higher education. It must be noted that a culture of "accountability" and culture of data are not the same thing. A culture of accountability is often prompted by external forces such as accreditors or reporting mandates. Although such a culture may be effective in the short term, it is difficult for an organization to develop and advance due to the impetus stemming from external forces rather than internal ones.

Stakeholders tend to be resistant to the requirements forced upon them, cutting into their already busy schedules. If there is no evidence of accountability data being used to make improvements, stakeholders become resentful. Further, accountability initiatives tend to focus on specific metrics of interest to external bodies rather than cohesive data of benefit to the institution and

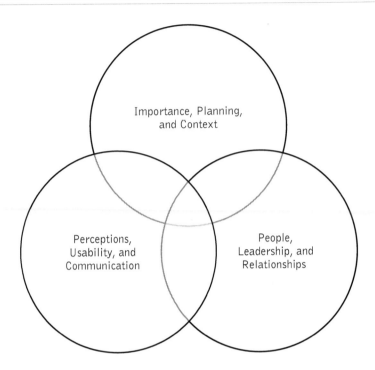

FIGURE 1.1 Elements of Data Culture.

ultimately student success. This narrow focus ignores data, which may be valuable in a broader context.

Lastly, a culture of accountability often involves only individuals at the upper levels of the institution and does not encourage data integration and discussion throughout the institution. In contrast, a data culture seeks to democratize and distill data into information to guide decision-making that focuses on the institution's mission.

WHY CULTIVATE A DATA CULTURE?

Benefits

While large companies that have arguably earned the title of "data leader" such as Google, Amazon, Facebook, LinkedIn, Walmart, FedEx, UPS, and General Electric rely on data to maintain a competitive edge, this approach has not been common in higher education, despite clear advantages to be gained in improved competitiveness from using data. Benefits of a strong data culture include improved communication and understanding of institutional metrics and trends.

While many people do not like to discuss the revenue side the equation, the fact is that presidents are expected to have a balanced budget. And no senior leader is pro-deficit. Organizations that successfully use data realize more growth than their counterparts that are not using data effectively.

For example, "Retailers who leverage the full power of big data could increase their operating margins by as much as 60%" (Marr, 2015, p. 1). Consider a public health example, "Estimates suggest that by better integrating big data, healthcare could save as much as $300 billion a year—that's equal to reducing costs by $1000 a year for every man, woman, and child" (Marr, 2015, p. 1). Given that organizations are achieving these results using 0.5% of collected data is amazing (Marr, 2015). Imagine the progress higher education institutions could make in the areas of student success and cost containment by using a fraction of the remaining 99.5% of collected data.

The public outcry over increased higher education costs has led to greater scrutiny of institutional resources. Thus, there is not only an incentive to having a strong and positive data culture, but there is also a risk of not having a data culture.

Risks of Not Having a Data Culture

Institutions tend to be data rich and information poor, awash with data points but yet lacking processes to transform that data into actionable insight. This disconnect prompts decision makers, who don't have time to devote to unraveling the web of data, to make choices based on isolated strands of data drawn from the mass. In short, institutions without a data culture make decisions without knowing the whole story. Such decisions have the potential to have substantial impact upon students, faculty, staff, alumni, and prospective students, to name just a few. Without a cohesive data culture in place, decisions with widespread implications are made in isolation and campus mythologies seep into the decision-making process, influencing outcomes.

CHARACTERISTICS OF A SUCCESSFUL DATA CULTURE

A successful data culture exhibits four key behaviors, it: 1) shares data, 2) values data, 3) trusts data, and 4) uses data. Figure 1.2. shows example strategies for each of these characteristics.

Shares Data

Transparency and access to data are key characteristics of a successful data culture. Patil and Mason (2015) advocated "everyone in an organization should

Shares Data
•Encourages data transparency •Provides access to data for all stakeholders •Makes data available to consumers outside the institution (prospective students, parents, etc.)

Values Data
•Appoints a chief data officer to ensure data expertise at leadership level •Makes data an intentional part of meetings and discussions •Ensures data from different sources are validated for accuracy and consistency

Trusts Data
•Allows conversations to progress based on confidence in data quality •Relies on data to establish appropriate benchmarks and goals •Inspires data use and diminishes user hesitancy

Uses Data
•Makes data discussions an expectation •Requires evidence to support suggestions and actions •Integrates data into institutional planning processes

FIGURE 1.2 Characteristics and Behaviors of Successful Data Cultures.

have access to as much data as legally possible" (p. 6). In an environment where access to data is easily granted rather than withheld, stakeholders are more likely to feel empowered to use data. Of course, granting access alone is only one piece of the equation; data themselves must be accessible to users as well. In this respect, it is critical that data systems and reports allow intuitive interpretation. Lacking this, stakeholders may feel that while they can access the data, they can't make sense of it, prompting them to retreat from data use. For infrequent data users, data should be humanized and contextualized to foster understanding.

Values Data

Integration of data review in recurring meetings maintains an emphasis on the importance of data at the institution. Rather than simply providing attendees with a report, time is set aside at the start of each meeting for data review and discussion. This ensures not only awareness of current data, but also that all involved have a shared understanding and interpretation of the data. This practice reiterates that data are an inherent part of discussions and decision-making. Value can be further demonstrated by the creation of a dedicated chief data officer role within the institution. This not only elevates the importance of data to an executive level, but also ensures that an individual with data proficiency is included in key discussions.

Trusts Data

Trust is critical to a successful data culture. Without it, gaining buy-in from institutional users is nearly impossible. Institutions with strong data cultures understand that data quality is the key to establishing broad data use. Weathington (2016) acknowledged lack of trust in data quality as "the number one reason why people are reluctant to rely on data" (p. 1). Trustworthy data do not happen overnight or without effort. Resources must be devoted to data cleansing and validation and supported by processes that emphasize the importance of data quality. In the absence of such processes, we return to the "garbage in, garbage out" mantra.

Validation of multiple data sources is another substantial task, but one that must be undertaken to ensure consistent data quality. While definitional issues will always result in a slight variation across reports, efforts should be made to ensure that these variations are clearly labeled and explained. This strengthens the perception that although data may differ, there is a legitimate reason for the variation. Whenever possible, data providers should use shared definitions to ensure consistent data.

Uses Data

All the effort of sharing and validating data is wasted if the data are not used. As Patil and Mason (2015) observed, many entities fall victim to the "if we build it, they will come" attitude, expecting data development work to result in immediate and extensive use. For data to be used, and used effectively, it must meet the needs of institutional stakeholders.

ASSESSING INSTITUTIONAL READINESS FOR A DATA CULTURE

Now that we have highlighted the advantages to establishing a data culture, the next obvious question is how to begin such an undertaking. It must first be noted that a data culture is not defined solely by the presence of data across an institution. While collecting data is simple, "it's what your organization does with data, however, which defines the culture" (Stringfellow, 2016, Harris section, para. 3). Prior to implementing steps toward a data culture, it is necessary to evaluate the current level of data literacy. One way to gain an understanding of the current state of the culture is to survey the campus community regarding its perception and use of data. Some sample questions to guide assessment of the current culture are shown in Figure 1.3. As discussed in depth in Chapter 2, understanding institutional culture and perceptions is critical. Conducting an audit to gain insight into existing perceptions regarding data not only

Perceptions of data:

- I think it is important to use data to inform decision-making.
- I like to use data.
- I feel comfortable using data.
- I feel comfortable interpreting data.
- I find data confusing and difficult to understand.
- I know where to get data necessary for my position.
- I have access to all the data I need to do my job.
- Data I have access to are easy to use.
- Data I have access to are easy to understand.
- Data available to me are useful.
- I know who to ask if I have questions about data.
- I receive sufficient training on data use.
- I prefer to receive data as a finished report.
- I prefer to receive raw data and analyze it myself.

Frequency of data use:

- How often do you use each of the following campus data systems/reports?
    - Student information system
    - HR information system
    - Course scheduling system
    - Reports created by Information Technology
    - Reports created by Institutional Research
- What are your primary concerns or frustrations with existing data systems and structures?

FIGURE 1.3 Questions to Guide Assessment of the Current Data Culture.

inherently validates data-informed planning (what could be more data-centric than collecting data on data use to inform planning of a data culture?), but also provides baseline data for future assessment.

Data collected from such an audit can be used to identify areas within the institution that will require a significant allocation of time and resources in the pursuit of a data culture. All units within the institution must be led to see the value of data and making decisions from a data evidenced perspective; some will require more guidance in this endeavor than others. Stringfellow (2016) noted that individuals faced with a shift to a data culture tend to have two chief concerns: "the first is that they will be scrutinized (and potentially punished) because everything is being measured more publicly. The second is the concern that becoming more numbers-focused will cause it to feel like a less personal work environment" (Marcotte section, para. 2).

While a strong data culture advantages all institutional stakeholders, do not expect overwhelming support at the outset of the initiative; Weathington (2016) suggested that approximately three-quarters of stakeholders do not place a high value on data initially.

ORGANIZATIONAL CHANGE

Cultivation of a data culture is most easily grounded in a teleological frame of organizational change. That is, organizational change which is intentional and flexible. Within this framework, change is fostered by leaders or advocates who understand the value of change and rely on institutional context to guide progress (Kezar, 2001). Situated within the teleological framework, organizational development is a widely used change strategy in higher education, perhaps because it "tends to address first-order change and does not challenge current organizational paradigms" (Kezar, 2001, p. 33). In such models, the role of change agents is significant in attaining successful organizational growth.

Organizational change does not happen at a quick pace, especially within higher education. The keys to attaining any lasting change are patience and persistence. This is especially true in relation to a data culture; not only do the typical organizational change resistances apply, but they are also compounded by institutional resistance to data.

PRACTICAL SUGGESTIONS AND GUIDANCE

- *Conduct a data culture audit.* Know where you are starting from. Identifying key goals, concerns, and roadblocks up front will help guide processes.
- *Designate a change agent to shepherd organizational change.* The level of the person selected will signal to the institution the level of importance; choose wisely. Note this does not need to be a data expert, but rather a person who is known for results, relationship building, and getting others to follow him/her through motivation as opposed to authority.
- *Ensure broad awareness and shared understanding of key metrics.* This is a time investment that will pay off when the entire institution—faculty, staff, and students—understands the key metrics. That which matters is measured.
- *Emphasize the benefits and advantages to be gained from data-informed decisions.* This may seem like stating the obvious, but if it were clear to everyone, campus stakeholders would already be using data more (and you wouldn't be reading this book).
- *Encourage employee use of data.* When creating a culture of data, more than a select group of people need to have access to use the data.

9

- *Engage with employees on the possibilities of data.* Create discussion forums to discuss uses and challenges of the data. This cross-sharing of information will allow employees to see new possibilities of using the data, thus going further and faster with data than before.
- *Educate employees on how to manipulate and use data.* Task existing data experts with educating other employees on how to analyze and prepare data for decision makers.
- *Make data usable.* "Get the data out of Excel and into a format that everyone can understand without manipulation. People want the answers that the data can provide; they just don't want to be the one that has to get it" (Stringfellow, 2016, Gardner section, para. 3).

SUMMARY

Cultivating a data culture is much more than committing to collecting all data points possible. Collecting data and doing nothing with it is bordering on negligence because all of the resources (data, people with know-how, time, etc.) exist to improve student success and institutional challenges. To collect without utilizing is simple a waste of resources. In fact, it would have been cheaper not to collect the information at all, if the data will remain dormant.

Recognizing that institutions are collecting more data than they are using and want to be more efficient with resources, this chapter focused on the pros and cons of cultivating a data culture. Assuming that one is interested in using data to advance the institution, we describe important characteristics of a data culture along with practical tips and considerations for implementation.

DISCUSSION QUESTIONS

1. Select one pro and one con of cultivating a data culture. Describe how each would be perceived at your institution (or an institution that you want to work at). Which one (pro or con) outweighs the other?
2. Of the characteristics of a data culture described in this chapter, which one is paramount to have? Why?
3. This chapter defined a data culture. How would you edit the definition to customize it for your institution?
4. Select two items from the practical suggestions and guidance section that you feel your institution (or institutions in general) need to focus on.
5. Imagine that you are charged with conducting an audit of your institution's data culture. What are three elements/areas that you would focus on?

REFERENCES

Kezar, A. J. (2001). *Understanding and facilitating organizational change in the 21st century: Recent research and conceptualizations*, Vol. 28(4). San Francisco, CA: Jossey-Bass Publishers.

Marr, B. (2015, September 30). Big data: 20 mind-boggling facts everyone must read. *Forbes.* Retrieved from www.forbes.com/sites/bernardmarr/2015/09/30/big-data-20-mind-boggling-facts-everyone-must-read/#3148c6e017b1.

Patil, D. J., & Mason, H. (2015). *Data-Informed: Creating a data culture.* Sebastopol, CA: O'Reilly. Retrieved from www.oreilly.com/data/free/data-informed.csp.

Stringfellow, A. (2016, January 19). How to create a data-driven culture: Tips from 33 experts. *NG Data.* Retrieved from www.ngdata.com/creating-a-data-informed-culture/.

Weathington, J. (2016, June 3). How to build a data-informed culture with credibility. *TechRepublic.* Retrieved from www.techrepublic.com/article/how-to-build-a-data-informed-culture-with-credibility/.

Chapter 2

Linking Planning, Ownership, Governance, and Execution

Fundamental Steps in Building an Effective Data Culture

Jason F. Simon, P. Daniel Chen, and Ah Ra Cho

INTRODUCTION

Despite the fact that institutions of higher education are awash in data, and that this volume of data is likely to increase further, Bichsel (2012) found most institutions of higher education have not yet fully realized the analytic potential of a robust data landscape. Given the slow pace at which higher education responds to change, only a few years later, Reinetz (2015) stated that: "higher education is data rich but information poor" (p. 4). Realizing that future growth in data competency is predicated on leveraging institutional data differently, institutions are now focusing on the need to approach their data in new ways. Reporting of official, often static, information as the norm is no longer good enough for modern higher education institutions. True value from a data landscape occurs when the institution can leverage existing data to answer problems focused on the future. Higher education administrators and stakeholders need an evolution in thinking that views assessment and institutional data not simply for accreditation purposes to close loops between practice and outcomes, but rather leverages data to create new loops for students to succeed with less barriers and in a quicker time-span (Zinshteyn, 2016).

Recognizing these demands, campus leadership, institutional governing boards, and state/federal agencies are pushing institutions to improve outcomes and establish new parameters for success (Ekowo & Palmer, 2017). The competitive marketplace is evolving and applying pressure on traditional institutions. There is a need for faster and more fundamental change and the speed of innovation is real and disrupting the status quo (Christensen & Eyring, 2011). Often these pressures manifest in the form of the establishment of enterprise-wide data warehouses, analytic solutions, data visualization tools, and the reallocation of existing IT resources to attempt to enact a quick fix from a data perspective. These efforts to bridge the chasm between terabytes of data and the complex solutions needed to tackle multifaceted and complex challenges facing our students, faculty, and institutions are vitally important. That being said, institutions will never be truly effective, if the focus is solely on tools and technology alone. Institutions of higher education are made up of faculty, staff, students, and alumni. These groups all contribute to an organization's data culture and influence prioritization activities.

Birnbaum (1988) describes culture broadly by the manner in which individuals think, act, and engage with one another. These interactions then in turn influence the broader community. This is a continuous process that serves as a foundation for how parts of the whole approach challenges and new solutions. A pitfall exists when consideration of institutional culture is ignored. Peter Drucker was quoted as saying "Culture eats strategy for breakfast" (Coffman & Sorenseon, 2013). Higher education should take note of the truth behind this assertion. At best, institutions that ignore culture open themselves up to risks associated with adoption of temporary fixes for persistent problems. At worst, institutions which overlook the power of culture risk sinking a tremendous amount of precious resources into a largely inadequate solution that may never be embraced by the members of the organization.

Creating a data-informed decision-making process in higher education institutions is very challenging. Data initiatives can become sidetracked by prioritization disagreements, ownership conflicts, turf wars, confusion over data responsibility, and a lack of formalized roles and responsibilities around data governance and management.

Confronting these issues requires planning and a conscious decision for the institution to reflect on current behaviors and norms. Linking planning to culture means paying attention to the people, processes, programs, and spoken and unspoken rules around a given data project in a given environment (department, division, campus, college, university, system, etc.). Culture-centric data leaders recognize the human element of their work. These leaders approach data prioritization with a different set of assumptions and practices that value the role of people, processes, and structures. That being said, we realize that not all institutions will have the same access to resources, staffing, and infrastructure. This chapter provides a baseline of best practices that institutions would do well to consider within their own unique organizational setting.

ASSESSING INSTITUTIONAL DATA PRIORITIES

Identify and Engage an Executive Champion

A culture-centric leader does not underestimate the impact of an executive champion on setting and influencing institutional data priorities. Executive champions are typically the chief executive officer, president, or chancellor.

13

Enthusiastic support from senior leadership within colleges and universities is more important than ever. It is widely shown that leadership is a key differentiator in determining success for data related projects (Grajek, 2016; Futhey, 2015; Zeid, 2014). Organizations that develop plans to solicit early and continued support for data projects with champions reap the benefit of the investment of time in this effort. Given the diverse array of data on campuses, projects will need a champion who can prioritize and determine the eventual implementation sequencing. Succeeding in the data marketplace today requires executive champions with specific goals in mind for their institutions. Seeking out his/her opinions of the strengths, weaknesses, opportunities, and threats around the institution's data landscape is a crucial first step. This is important especially if your culture is in opposition to these expectations. Executive champions also play crucial roles in data governance and data management decisions if the campus is operating in a diffuse data environment with numerous systems, definitions, and data sources. This is the perfect opportunity for an executive champion to help address ambiguous or contested data practices. Ultimately, an executive champion is very helpful in influencing culture change on items that have historically been fuzzy or unclear to the wider institutional community.

Conduct a Data Maturity and Analytics Climate Audit

In order to assess institutional data priorities in specific detail, culture-centric data leaders must first prioritize time to assess the larger institutional data culture that influences these priorities. Achieving this goal requires substantive conversations about the maturity of an institution's campus culture when it comes to data and increasingly the leveraging of data for analytic purposes. In its most simple form, data maturity is the capacity for an organization or campus to achieve maximum benefit from data-related assets. These assets will either hamper or accelerate outcomes from prioritization activities. Zeid (2014) asserted that these assets include people, processes, technical infrastructure, and culture. In a mature organization, these assets align to achieve maximum analytic efficiency, discover innovative solutions to common organizational challenges, and deliver better solutions and services to constituents.

Figure 2.1 represents the stages of data maturity and highlights how an organization evolves into more advanced states around information evolution (Zeid, 2014) and data prioritization. Use of this model assesses information and analytical maturity, helps to indicate a future direction for a campus, prioritizes engagement in projects that deliver maximum value to both institutions and students, and guides both short-term and long-term steps to achieve strategic goals. Furthermore, this model places the best interests of the institution/ enterprise over the individual needs of a given department.

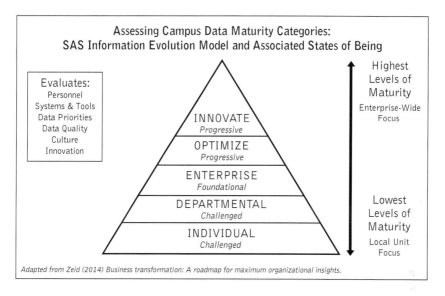

FIGURE 2.1 SAS Information Evolution Model.

Zeid's 2014 classifications for campus data maturity offer a quick opportunity for a baseline campus culture audit and focuses leaders on data prioritization activities that go beyond individual data domains, types, or silos.

Individual Categorization

Campuses in the individual state of maturity will see numerous data examples of the institution focusing on immediate and tactical needs or consumed with responding to present-day ad hoc data needs. These campuses have operations focusing on daily activities and generating static reports at regular time intervals. Data are largely used to track or manage day-to-day operations in key business areas and are often stored in narrow "stovepipe" applications or transactional student information systems. Unfortunately for campuses that find themselves in this category, data are most often leveraged to make decisions after events have already transpired, providing limited impact on the true concerns. Zeid (2014) considered these organizations in a challenged state of being. Data priorities are often determined by the loudest voice, the individual with most seniority, or the area that has taken the time to embed their work in institutional policy. All data are equally important in these environments and, as such, no forward progress can be made to innovate for the greater institution's benefits.

Departmental Categorization

Campuses in the departmental maturity category will be typified by student, academic, finance, and advancement operations that primarily focus on individual department data metrics and showcasing individual impacts. In this state, Zeid (2014) recognized that entire departments might be savvy when it comes to data, yet this is not consistent across the entire organization. These pockets of subject matter experts (SMEs) are incredibly valuable to the department. Senior leadership usually has concerns should an SME retire or pursue employment elsewhere. These institutions prioritize localized departmental level data processes to govern their student, academic, or financial data. Once again, data priorities are established in isolation and mirror the ways the actual data are stored—in silos. Teams, according to Zeid (2014), are aware there could be better ways of operating, but they lack the tools, technology, or training to break down silos on the campus. These organizations breed leadership concerns around data veracity. The lack of enterprise-wide prioritization causes concerns about multiple versions of the truth in the data. Zeid (2014) also considers these organizations to be in a challenged state.

Enterprise Categorization

Campuses in the enterprise category begin to balance between individual departmental data needs and enterprise-wide data needs. These institutions prioritize investing in data sources, tools, and technology to benefit a majority of campus users, units, departments, etc. The overall institution begins to rely on data to solve complex challenges. Key Performance Indicators (KPIs) are in use and regularly monitored across campus. The campus not only recognizes the inherent value of data but also prioritizes it as an asset (Zeid, 2014). Data now drives goals and offers insights into growth opportunities for the campus. Data prioritization is no longer based on the loudest voice or the most critical burning question. Instead, data prioritization results from formalized data definitions and business rules. Metadata (data about data) should be readily available, if a concern about validity arises. Data governance groups meet with purpose to help provide structure to enterprise-wide data prioritization and leaders trust these processes. These campuses are now considered by Zeid (2014) as having achieved a foundational level of analytic maturity and are beginning to break away from the ungoverned and fractured data landscapes in higher education.

Optimized Categorization

Campuses in the optimized category are typified by a set of systems that are designed for data automation in the analytics arena. Interactive, user-defined, and automatically refreshed dashboards allow campus constituents and leaders to move the organization forward. Executive sponsors prioritize valid external data to bring to bear on the challenges facing the organization. Labor statistics, state demographer data, federal database extracts, and local municipal data are commonly utilized to make decisions. Use of unstructured data (social media, internet of things, wearables, etc.) is commonplace within these institutions and an expansion of offerings and campus programming results from the better data present. Zeid (2014) also posits that an intentional focus on providing value to students, parents, and constituents drives the organization forward. This value proposition makes data prioritization conversations far simpler. Systems that are redundant or not delivering value to the community are staged for eventual phase out. These are truly innovative campus cultures. While only a select few institutions of higher education may exist in this category, it is certainly the aspiration of governing boards and institutional stakeholders that our institutions achieve this state of being. Zeid (2014) considers these institutions to be in a progressive state.

Innovative Categorization

These are considered to be the pinnacle of data-informed campuses driven by analytics. These are proactive institutions, which place a priority on continuous improvement in all areas of campus. Individual contributions from data SMEs are highly recognized and rewarded. External data are easily consumed and leveraged for rapid decision-making. Data-informed decision-making virtually assures dominance as a leader within higher education. In these organizations, traditional staff hierarchies are eschewed for outcome-driven work groups, who, based on their technical competencies and acumen, are organized to solve complex problems regardless of reporting lines (Zeid, 2014).

Culture-centric leaders set on improving data prioritization can do so by examining this model and engaging in spirited conversations across a campus to determine where the institution falls on the maturity spectrum. We recognize that some pockets of the institution may be further along the continuum than others. In those instances, culture-centric leaders should seek to ask themselves if these pockets truly represent the totality of the campus or are outliers. The key here is to have a solid understanding of how overall data maturity is related to prioritization and culture. These conversations and insights represent a powerful tool in one's arsenal that enables culture-centric leaders to press forward with the work of improving the data landscape through new initiatives focused on improving the state of the institution's overall data maturity.

Stakeholder Identification, Assessment, and Engagement

Identifying stakeholders is an important consideration when moving from overall institutional data prioritization to individual subject matter areas. Stakeholders are often identified by seeking out those responsible or accountable for data and colleagues who are often consulted or informed about data developments. This is accomplished through the process formally known as a Responsible, Accountable, Consulted, or Informed (RACI) exercise (see below for a more detailed explanation of the benefits of RACI) or by leveraging existing source documents (IT charters, taskforce findings, etc.) on campus to identify subject matter experts (SMEs) or technical SMEs.

It is important to note that stakeholders within the college or university community have unique approaches to, and interest in, adapting to new data tools. For any data prioritization activity to be effective, culture-centric leaders tasked with planning for and executing new tools should be cognizant that the college or university community will not react homogenously. Instead, as posited by Rogers (1995), individuals will fall into various adoption categories: innovators, early adopters, early majority, late majority, and laggards. Ensuring that these voices are present in planning processes is an important step in ensuring diverse stakeholder opinions are heard.

Once identified, a solid planning technique is to build relationships with these individuals, gain their trust through genuine collegiality, and eventually assess their thoughts and opinions regarding common data frustrations on campus (see Figure 2.2). While knowing what is done well matters, looking intentionally at frustration builds consensus for change, validates data prioritization concerns, and addresses the main problem for many campuses—the disconnect between data and the work involved in managing it. This assessment also provides campus leadership with quantitative data on stakeholder sentiment from those in the trenches and serves as a guidepost to evaluate future vendor solutions against documented concerns and frustrations. This exercise ultimately puts data prioritization into context by measuring the severity of challenges facing any data source at the institution.

A final stakeholder engagement strategy is to leverage an annual data summit. Working in partnership with stakeholders across campus, bring SMEs and technical SMEs together for a focused summit on the state of your institution's data. What is available? What is needed? What was learned by the frustration index? Where are improvements needed in terms of data tools, processes, or governance? The summit provides excellent opportunities for individuals who may work regularly with each other on isolated data challenges to have time to think on a larger scale about the needs of the institution. Getting the data teams out of their units and gathering them all together fosters a renewed spirit around the

_____ is tasked with addressing the need to improve the data
landscape across _____. In order to help improve a system or process it is often
helpful to begin first with common frustrations. Please share with us your reactions to the
statements below by marking the appropriate bubble. Please note that this is anonymous.
**In thinking about the data you need or manage to do your job, how frustrated are
you with the following common data challenges?**

ITEM	Never a Frustration	Somewhat a Frustration	Growing Frustration	Consistent Frustration	N/A
The data have not been collected.	O	O	O	O	
I don't know where the data are located.	O	O	O	O	
I don't know who owns or has the data.	O	O	O	O	
I don't know if the data are actually in our possession.	O	O	O	O	
I don't know when the data are pulled/refreshed.	O	O	O	O	
I don't know if I'm processing the data correctly.	O	O	O	O	
I don't know if the data are accurate.	O	O	O	O	
If I own the data, I don't have the time to validate it.	O	O	O	O	O
Other:	O	O	O	O	
Other:	O	O	O	O	
Other:	O	O	O	O	

I primarily: O Working in my area's data/data tables, coding, programming, writing/using
spend most   SQL, etc.
of my time: O Working to help leadership understand my area's data and/or data related
                     outcomes
                  O Working across both of these roles almost equally

FIGURE 2.2 Sample Questions to Gauge SME and Stakeholder Data Frustration
Index. Source: Simon, 2016.

campus data culture. This event provides leadership with a forum to innovate
and to lay out a critical path forward for new ways of approaching data prioritization. Having these conversations take place without the burden of the latest
data emergency to solve supports the collective potential of stakeholders to
improve our institutional data outcomes.

Keeping Prioritization Personal—Individual Assessment

Putting personal bias aside is a challenging yet necessary task for individuals to engage in the work of assessing data priorities. Likewise, having a realistic self-appraisal around skills, competencies, and tools related to data is also needed. In addition to fostering an environment where practitioners can learn, grow, and experience data professional development activities, campuses should also establish tools to help faculty, staff, and administrators assess their own data competencies. Gemignani, Gemignani, Galentino, and Schuermann (2014) encourage individuals to think critically about their own level of proficiency around the use of data, data tools, data manipulation skills, the value they place on data at the organization, and how their own perceptions and attitudes about data permeate their thinking about campus culture. They argue that this intro-spective process is highly instructive for leaders grappling with how to help an organization evolve its thinking regarding data prioritization. Equally as important, leaders in higher education who work with data must have the ability not only prioritize data but also explain the implications of these decisions and the stories behind these choices. This is one final area where data prioritization can either be helped or hampered by an individual's skills. Lefever (2013) describes this ability to tell stories as the art of explanation. Becoming a story-teller around data prioritization is a vital skill (and is discussed in detail in Chapter 12). Fortunately, this is a skill that can be nurtured, if culture-centric data leaders take the necessary steps to focus differently on the roles they play in helping their campus move forward in an ever-evolving and rapidly changing data landscape.

DETERMINING OWNERSHIP AND DATA PRIORITIZATION

Data prioritization is complicated by confusion around ownership. While data governance practices described below bring additional clarity, a key first step is to categorize the roles which individuals play in the data landscape. These cate-gorizations bring clarity to often unclear roles and responsibilities. The time spent on working through this process with stakeholders is very beneficial to the overall data management process.

Eduventures (2013) found that as "colleges and universities have slowly adapted to technology over time, many have five, ten, or even more discrete systems collecting data" (p. 6). Given this diversity, and in some cases disparity, it is important that stakeholders who represent these systems remain engaged in meaningful ways. Determining ownership begins with a broad examination of the total data landscape. This can be accomplished by working with stakeholders or partners in Institutional Research, Business Intelligence, or Information

Technology to document and distribute an inventory of all of the major data sources and systems on campus. One needs to also consider non-traditional data sources such as areas in facilities, libraries, advancement, institutional effectiveness, etc. The benefit of starting with the system first and not with the owner ensures that culture-centric data leaders think holistically about their data landscapes.

Once a master list of data sources and systems is created, this documents the people, departments, and stakeholders involved in ensuring that the data and system is successful. It is also very wise to engage information security, legal counsel, or the organization's policy office. On many campuses, data ownership is often a proxy for data security. Recognizing the role security plays in the ownership process early on may eliminate confusion and promote quicker movement through this phase of documenting people resources. This is typically where most higher education ownership conversations stop. Unfortunately, by not pushing ahead, role confusion may remain and when data problems arise the certainty of ownership is still in question. Rather, culture-centric leaders should use a process tool known as a RACI matrix to partner with leadership and stakeholders to assign individuals into four major categories as outlined by Kantor (2012):

- *Responsible (R)*: Stakeholders who at the end of the day are tasked with doing the work with either the data or the data system.
- *Accountable (A)*: Stakeholders who decide and act on a set of given tasks within the data or data system.
- *Consulted (C)*: Stakeholders who will be kept engaged as work and decisions are needed within the data domain or system.
- *Informed (I)*: Stakeholders who will get regular updates throughout the course of the work (as these efforts influence or impact their ability to use data or data systems).

Working to classify stakeholders into these categories by data source or data system proactively eliminates confusion. Marketing these categorizations elevates the transparency of data on campus and eliminates the inefficiency of tracking down the "right place" to resolve a data issue. Revisiting the RACI matrix on an annual basis ensures that the organization is maintaining accurate data owners and influencers. When done well and managed properly, a RACI activity highlights risks, opportunities, and strengths in a data landscape. It also serves as a powerful document to influence change and move priorities forward during times of challenge. Once completed, culture-centric leaders can design segment specific communications and updates about systems and challenges.

CHECKS AND BALANCES FOR SUCCESS: LEVERAGING DATA GOVERNANCE PRACTICES

Advances gained from data governance structures in other industries such as health care, banking, and commerce have not arrived to the sector of higher education. We must recognize that there is no longer a simple way to control data or to ensure a single version of the truth exists on a campus where numerous data stakeholders may utilize a wide range of datasets and tools (Swing & Ross, 2016). Culture-centric data leaders recognize that investing time in learning more about data governance is not only important but is also increasingly strategically necessary. The Privacy Technical Assistance Center (PTAC) (n.d.) defines data governance "as an organizational approach to data and information management that is formalized as a set of policies and procedures that encompass the full life cycle of data, from acquisition to use to disposal" (pp. 1–2). Engaging campuses in robust data governance processes force institutions to confront unspoken norms, tackle ownership issues, and define the operating principles for how various data users throughout campus will need to behave with one another. Figure 2.3 highlights the various components of an effective data governance effort.

It is important to note that the mission and vision referred to above in Figure 2.3 do not relate to campus mission and vision. Rather, this is the mission and vision for the data governance program. Determining goals, metrics for success, and a budget to complete this work is a baseline requirement. Recognizing even

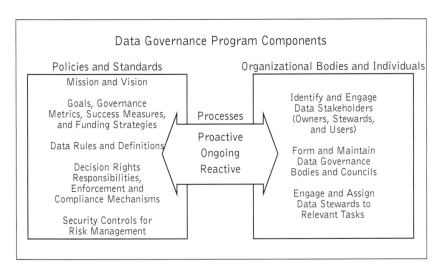

FIGURE 2.3 Data Governance Program Components (Adapted from the Privacy Technical Assistance Center).

the soft-costs of staff involved in a data governance project is important, even if the institution is not prepared to invest new dollars from budgeted funds. Working on who has the right to make changes to data (decision rights), who has the responsibility to uphold these decisions, tasked by virtue of policy or service level agreements (codified requirements and timelines to resolve data issues between parties), and who will monitor all the work so that the institution does not violate student privacy, or state or federal law are all important considerations.

Work teams also need to consider how processes serve as a crucial linking agent to connect policies and standards with organizational bodies and individuals. These processes require documentation and forethought so that they can be responsive to data needs before they occur. Also, they need to promote stability through ongoing and repeatable steps and be nimble enough to respond to emergencies, data breaches, etc. Developing these processes will be long and protracted at first, yet the campus will gain efficiencies as the practices take hold in the culture of the data landscape.

The final area to consider is the actual organizational bodies needed to implement this process. Who will be tasked with participating from the stakeholders? How often will the group meet and where? What tools or mechanisms will be used to track work product and results? Arriving at responses to these questions will take time and vision. The culture-centric data leader understands the investment in time of documenting a RACI matrix and identifying key stakeholders pays dividends at this point in time. If the policies and standards are the skeleton, and the processes are the organs, then the organizational bodies and people are surely the central nervous system of an effective data governance process.

Ultimately, institutions with strong data governance programs have individuals specifically tasked with leading these efforts. While campuses will have data owners, data stewards, or data user groups, often an administrative infrastructure is missing from a program coordination perspective. Given the advances in data management tools on the market, having a dedicated professional staff member with the acumen to run a data governance program is important. Ideally, this individual should have a combination of both practical data management and data organization experience, and either a background in higher education data systems or a track record of being able to quickly come to speed in learning new data landscapes. Institutional leaders in this space have defined roles and responsibilities that task them with building out or maintaining data governance efforts and initiatives. These leaders should have the support of the executive champion as a necessary ally in this process. The PTAC (n.d.) stresses that data governance programs must focus on clarifying decision-making authority, ensuring that specific and measurable data standards are in place, and having a framework for facilitating data management process are not only readily available but are also easily understood.

Data governance is not and will not be easy to execute. It requires patience, persistence, and the willingness to slowly impact a data culture that may take years, if not decades, to fully implement. Campuses who engage in this work should allow ample time to reach a state of maturity and be amenable that the process of data governance is just as important as the final outcomes. Data governance does put appropriate pressures on the overall system to maintain data quality, veracity, and privacy (Gorman, 2014). When executed in a systematic and regular way, data governance serves as a perfect defense against the constant barrage of new ideas, the latest fads in technology, or the whims of a select few who want to rush into the next great solution. Data governance is a vital element of institutional capacity for measured change, when executed in a manner that promotes innovation while maintaining stability and promoting value to the institution (Gorman, 2014).

PRACTICAL SUGGESTIONS AND GUIDANCE

- *Gain insight into organizational culture.* Read as much as you can about differences in organizational culture between the various divisions of a higher education institution. Recognize that each division will have its own set of expectations, requirements, and needs from data and data tools.
- *Consider a data maturity audit.* Investigate if a data maturity audit has occurred or if you need to consider starting a process.
- *Review old IT project charters and white papers.* These can help to identify possible stakeholders, data pitfalls, and prioritization challenges from the past.
- *Start with a lunch.* Gather like-minded data colleagues from around campus to begin conversations around the ideal state of data on your campus. Develop some next steps to expand your circle of influencers.
- *Review executive sponsor concerns.* Examine press releases, internal communications, or formal requests to Institutional Research, Business Intelligence Units, or Information Technology to understand opportunities for engagement.
- *Examine peer campuses.* Where are they in their data governance efforts? Consider site visits to learn more and see different structures in action.
- *Take a course in storytelling.* Connect the seemingly disparate roles of data leader with storyteller to advance your organization through data prioritization activities.
- *Conduct a review of data policies and procedures.* Identify gaps and develop plans to partner with relevant campus units to address.
- *Understand the campus data culture.* Consider stakeholder focus groups, surveys, or other feedback gathering opportunities to build your understanding of the campus data culture.
- *Hold a data summit.* Provide the structure and the agenda but then listen—carefully.

CONCLUSION

Planning for any large-scale technology deployment, new initiative, or toolset requires more than just the traditional requirements of gathering work done in small isolated meetings to determine prioritization. Embracing or defying campus culture as part of the planning process will either improve or derail a data initiative or prioritization activity. This chapter has outlined several foundational planning tactics, which, if executed properly, will provide a robust and strong foundation to build upon and grow. Becoming a culture-centric data leader requires being willing and able to delay an immediate desire to push ahead without considering the people, tools, and processes already in existence on campus. Culture-centric data leaders take a step back and plan for change in a manner that embraces a campus culture and places the data prioritization conversation within a larger enterprise-wide data governance process.

DISCUSSION QUESTIONS

1. How would campus stakeholders describe the campus culture related to data?
2. Where does your campus fit in terms of data maturity and practice?
3. What strategies will you put in place to ensure that key constituents and stakeholders are effectively engaged in ways that are consistent with your campus culture?
4. What are some strategies you would utilize to engage an executive sponsor? How have previous projects engaged these individuals? What mechanisms would you put in place to encourage and foster his/her support through this process?
5. What data systems exist on your campus and where would individuals be categorized on a RACI matrix for each system?
6. How might you leverage data governance practices to improve the data prioritization and data quality of your campus?

REFERENCES

Bichsel, J. (2012). *Analytics in higher education: Benefits, barriers, progress, and recommendations.* Louisville, CO: EDUCAUSE Center for Applied Research.

Birnbaum, R. (1988). *How colleges work: The cybernetics of academic organization and leadership.* San Francisco, CA: Jossey-Bass.

Christensen, C. M. & Eyring, H. J. (2011). *The innovative university: Changing the DNA of higher education from the inside out.* San Francisco, CA: Jossey-Bass.

Coffman, C. & Sorenseon, K. (2013). *Culture eats strategy for lunch: The secret of extraordinary results, igniting the passion within.* Denver, CO: Liang Addison Press.

Eduventures (2013). *Predictive analytics in higher education: Data-informed decision-making for the student life cycle.* Boston, MA: Eduventures.

Ekowo, M. & Palmer, I. (2017, March 6). Predictive analytics in higher education: Five guiding practices for ethical use. *New America.* Retrieved from www.newamerica. org/education-policy/policy-papers/predictive-analytics-higher-education/#.

Futhey, T. (2015). IT Leadership. In A. Shark (Ed.), *The digital revolution in higher education: How and why the internet of everything is changing everything* (pp. 111–134). Alexandria, VA: Public Technology Institution.

Gemignani, Z., Gemignani, C., Galentino, R., & Schuermann, P. (2014). *Data fluency: Empowering your organization with effective data communication.* Indianapolis, IN: John Wiley & Sons.

Gorman, N. (2014). *The blueprint for a new HE data landscape: The higher education data and information improvement programme executive summary.* Retrieved from www.sfc. ac.uk/web/FILES/CMP_IGSCommittee4June2015_04062015/IGS_189_2015 _HEDIIP_Data_Landscape_Executive_Summary_item_10.pdf.

Grajek, S. (2016). Top 10 IT issues 2016: Divest, reinvest, and differentiate. *Educause Review, 51*(1).

Kantor, B. (2012). *How to design a successful RACI project plan. IDG communications.* Retrieved from www.cio.com/article/2395825/project-management/how-to-design-a-successful-raci-project-plan.html.

Lefever, L. (2013). *The art of explanation: Making your ideas, products, and services easier to understand.* Hoboken, NJ: John Wiley and Sons.

Privacy Technical Assistance Center (n.d.). *Data governance and stewardship.* Retrieved from https://nces.ed.gov/programs/ptac/pdf/issue-brief-data-governance-and-stewardship.pdf.

Reinetz, B. T. (2015). Building institutional analytics maturity. *October 2015 ECAR Summit Report.* Louisville, CO: EDUCAUSE.

Rogers, E. (1995). *Diffusion of innovations* (4th ed.). New York: Simon and Schuster.

Simon, J. (2016). *Data Frustration Index: Insights Program SME Feedback Gathering.* Denton, TX: University of North Texas.

Swing, R. L. & Ross, L. E. (2016). A new vision for institutional research. *Change: The Magazine of Higher Learning, 48*(2): 6–13.

Zeid, A. (2014). *Business transformation: A roadmap for maximizing organizational insights.* Hoboken, NJ: John Wiley and Sons.

Zinshteyn, M. (2016, November 1). The colleges are watching. *The Atlantic.* Retrieved from www.theatlantic.com/education/archive/2016/11/the-colleges-are-watching/506129/.

Chapter 3

Using Context to Maximize the Utility of Data

Michael M. Black

INTRODUCTION

More higher education administrators outside of the Institutional Research Office are utilizing data to make important strategic decisions. While this is commendable, these individuals should have sound knowledge of the environmental background of the institution before attempting to interpret the data. The complexity of a higher education institution often means that context is poorly used, however, Swanson and Rinehart (2016, p. 97) stated clearly, "Data needs context". Frequently said, data without context is meaningless.

As higher education institutions collect increasing amounts of data, many institutions believe they have "big data." However, Lorentz (2013) pointed out that it has "limited value if not paired with its younger and more intelligent sibling, context" (The Age of Context, para. 1). Although they may be technically proficient in their discipline, not all individuals will possess sufficient knowledge of an institution's rich history and culture in order to apply that knowledge correctly to data for strategic decisions. The real key to understanding data is knowing its context, and at some institutions, big data has failed due to the inadequate understanding and application of context to the data.

As baby boomers and Generation Xers exit the workplace, the new Generation Z is positioned to enter. The advantage of working at an institution for a long period of time is that one develops context, often soaking up more than one would think possible. However, when new employees start at an institution, they could potentially utilize big data to make decisions without clearly knowing context. Who will teach these new employees how to develop context so they can look to see what surrounds the numbers? Not only is context needed to improve the accuracy of interpreting data and making decisions, but as Knight shared, "understanding context is closely linked to people's ability to move up in the workplace. These are skills that can be learned over time" (2017, n.p.).

This chapter provides several definitions of context, multiple context scenarios, and issues about learning and working within an environment. Granted time with experience is the best way to gain context, this author concludes with several strategies for developing a deeper knowledge of institutional context that readers can leverage to get up to speed faster.

DEFINING CONTEXT AND UNDERSTANDING ITS VALUE

When describing foundations of context, Bouckaert (2013) shared the work of Gottlob Frege (1848–1925), a German mathematician and philosopher. Bouckaert (2013) stated,

> his fundamental methodological principles, which became known as Frege's context principle: never to ask for the meaning of a word in isolation, but only in the context of a proposition. According to this principle ... only in the context of a sentence do words have meaning (p. 74).

As higher education professionals, this concept also applies to the interpretation and utilization of any data, be it qualitative, quantitative, or a combination of both.

The ease of locating information on the Internet produces numerous definitions of context. As a noun, context is commonly defined as "the surroundings, circumstances, environment, background or settings that determine, specify, or clarify the meaning of an event or other occurrence" (Wiktionary, 2017, p. 1). Another definition, developed by Dey (2001) stated, "Context is any information that can be used to characterize the situation of an entity. An entity is a person, place, or object that is considered relevant to the interaction..." (p. 5).

Swanson and Rinehart (2016) affirmed,

> When the term data is placed within the context of specific types of research, disciplines, and needs, it becomes much easier to understand how the word is defined in that context, regardless of what it may mean in a different context (p. 97).

To some individuals, the word *context* itself can be off-putting, so other words, such as those shown in Figure 3.1, may be substituted.

Think about these words. If a supervisor or co-worker asks questions which use any of these words, he or she is seeking to expand his or her contextual knowledge. In order to be fully understood, individuals providing data should "operationalize [context] as a combination of pretext and post-text, of supra-text and infra-text, of internal text (footnotes, subtitles, surtitles) and external text (appendix, references)" (Bouckaert, 2013, p. 75).

- Background
- Characterization
- Circumstance
- Climate
- Condition
- Connection
- Demands
- Environment
- Expectations
- Frame of reference
- Framework
- Influences
- Milieu
- Requirements
- Scene
- Setting
- Situation
- State of affairs
- Surroundings
- Terrain

FIGURE 3.1 All of These Words Refer to Context.

While this book is designed to help inform and build a data culture among professionals outside traditional data fields, some long-established principles from the field of institutional research can easily be applied to other areas within higher education, even to disciplines outside of higher education. Terenzini (1993, 1999) developed three tiers of organizational intelligence as it relates to institutional research. The first tier is technical/analytical intelligence; the second tier is issues intelligence; and the third tier is contextual intelligence. Tier one consists of "factual knowledge or information and analytical and methodological skills and competencies" (Terenzini, 1999, p. 23).

Tier two entails "knowledge of the major issues or decision areas that face institutions and the people who manage them" (Terenzini, 1999, p. 24). Tier three, designated as the highest level of intelligence, requires an institutional researcher to know "the institution's historical and philosophical evolution, faculty and organizational cultures, informal as well as formal campus political structures and codes, governance, decision-making processes, and customs" (Terenzini, 1999, p. 25). Compared to tier one and tier two, tier three cannot typically be learned through formal study such as a textbook or seminar.

In 2013, Terenzini revisited the tiers. All three tiers remain relevant today, however, he made some modifications and additions, including expanding contextual intelligence to also include "subtler and more savvy political skills" (2013, p. 137). Now that context has been defined, the remainder of the chapter provides reflections and suggestions to practitioners about the sometimes nebulous concept of context.

LEARNING THE ENVIRONMENT

Questions answered in this section:

1. How can a practitioner learn about culture at an institution?
2. What is meant by current context and historical context?

When beginning a job at a new institution, one can easily become overwhelmed by a complex bureaucracy, and no doubt one which is prompted, or sometimes plagued, by numerous higher education initiatives. These initiatives likely surround the national college completion movement (i.e., retention, progression, and graduation), finances, or some other national or state political priorities. Many public institutions, particularly access and regional comprehensive institutions, try to "be everything to everybody every day" (Hill, Loshbaugh, Grote, & Arcarese, 2017, n.p.). With such a large spread of ideas, how can a practitioner begin learning the environment?

Consider this scenario in Figure 3.2.

Humans have generally been trained to believe that a right answer will almost always lead to a positive outcome. Higher education administrators need to

---

The institution is experiencing large enrollment gains and administrators have asked for research to be conducted and that a recommendation be made about the need for additional on-campus student housing. The final product includes a sound proposal backed by concrete data.

Interpretation without context: There is no way the executive team (president, vice-presidents) could not concur with the recommendation.

Interpretation with context: Executive leadership decides against the recommendation because of competing considerations, such as accounting for pressures on resources within the environment of which you are not aware (required implementation of new Title IX policies, for example) and the external political environment.

FIGURE 3.2 Context Scenario One.

begin to feel more comfortable in allowing data to lead them to the strategy or vision. Although they are often not trained in this way, they do need this attribute more than any other, particularly in the growing atmosphere of accountability in higher education (R. M. Zaccari, personal communication, February 17, 2017). It is incumbent upon any professional working in higher education to begin developing a certain knowledge about his or her employer and those individuals that comprise its workforce. Granted, attaining contextual intelligence skills can be achieved by reading an institution's written history, however, this author concurs with Terenzini (1999) in that the "knowledge comes from working on a campus for a number of years" (p. 27).

In addition to time, with practice, higher education administrators can obtain contextual intelligence, marked by the point when one "know[s] the environment in which their college or university operates and fully grasp[s] the opportunities and constraints presented" (Eimers, Ko, & Gardner, 2012, p. 46). Keeping this in mind, there is context which has immediate and current bearing and then there is also historical context. Current, or immediate, context is simply what is occurring at the present that will impact or inform a decision. Historical context is context which can be drawn from past events at a campus which will impact or inform a decision being made in the present. For example, consider a regional institution which began as a normal school (i.e., teacher preparation institution) to prepare public school teachers. This historical context helps to explain many present-day factors; two common results are that the institution likely has a high female enrollment and likely has a smaller endowment than comparable institutions, which did not begin as a normal school (Black, 2008). Quite often, high-level administrators who come to an institution and do not appreciate, or even attempt to understand, historical context regarding the institution and how things have developed will encounter difficulty with the implementation and adoption of major changes.

An information management study by Marcella and Knox (2004) found that higher education institutions "observ[ed] the rhetoric of requiring and producing a strategy without taking on board in spirit what was necessary for the strategy to be meaningful" (p. 3). When context is not fully connected to the data being used to develop a strategy or vision, the information can become impractical.

WORKING WITHIN THE ENVIRONMENT

The first rule of thumb for working within the environment is to actually work in the environment and not around the environment. Attempting to skirt around people or policies to achieve a goal has a potential for long-term violation of trust, honesty, and integrity. An administrator must understand formal and informal power structures, and this often relates to resource allocation. As a higher education administrator, creating an open climate for the exchange of information and ideas based on data is possible when making the best out of the current environment.

Consider this scenario in Figure 3.3.

Part of understanding context is learning and experiencing the institution's culture. Cultural characteristics include those beliefs, behaviors, and assumptions that are shared among the organization and have developed over time (Conner, 1992). Culture is more deeply rooted than solely based on a current president's vision and values (R. M. Zaccari, personal communication, February 17, 2017). Requirements and expectations at the national, state, and local levels including those of the university itself, down to school and departmental levels, all contribute to the campus culture and to the context by which administrators make decisions. Context also includes requirements of accreditation organizations as well as anything else within the environment historically, presently, or that is anticipated which could influence outcomes.

Performance has become a key operative idea within the university. This notion drives program improvement and reform and ultimately determines whether goals and objectives are met. Numbers are the quantified words of performance. Think of the number as a pebble, and the sling as its context. Each is necessary for the proper functioning of the slingshot as a whole. In a world of changing expectations and decreasing funding, "managing performance includes measuring and collecting performance data, embedding this data as performance information in documents, procedures and cycles, and ultimately using it to ensure that taking responsibility and being accountable for performance is substantial" (Bouckaert, 2013, p. 74).

A data-aware professional is responsible for making the institution and its president successful. This can be fostered by "influencing up" through providing data context to help senior leaders set expectations and make the institution more effective. Even opening a door slightly with an introduction such as,

---

Institutional enrollment must grow by 2% per year for at least 3 years to meet increases in anticipated expenses. Data consists of reports of enrollment trends for the past 10 years.

Interpretation without context: Expect to attract more applications to enroll more students.

Interpretation with context: The number of graduating high school seniors in the state is declining, and therefore, the pool of potential, traditional student applicants is decreasing. Plan for a potential budget cut and also seek outside the traditional student market to find a balance.

FIGURE 3.3 Context Scenario Two.

"Here are some things you need to know before you start to digest this data and make decisions based on the data …" can provide a contextual framework. By providing context to key decision makers, practitioners are positioning these decision makers to implement a decision that is congruent with the organization's culture (Conner, 1992). Once a decision has been made, senior leaders should continuously scan the environment for signals and be willing to change course mid-implementation. If staff are sending panic signals, pause and reassess (Hill et al., 2017).

CONNECTING CONTEXT TO DATA

In a public forum at a regional, comprehensive institution, a president said, "I value data but also understand the human dimension of decisions" (Brown, 2016). She was referring to context; use the data to inform a decision, yet couple it with those contextual factors, which are not reflected in the actual data. These are the plethora of factors and variables that a computer cannot graph or predict, but those that only a human mind can connect data to its surroundings. For example, there are certain numbers, such as applications for admission, that should move so an institution can progress and grow, but these numbers need to move in context to the institution. It is perhaps one element to voice that admission applications are up, but the why is as important as the how much. What intervention was made to increase admission applications? Conner (1992) summarized that all learning must precede change. Successful change occurs when synergy between data and context is created.

Consider this scenario in Figure 3.4.

Data consist of numbers. Numbers result from measuring. Numbers without a frame of reference (or context) are meaningless. How well practitioners

---

The institution's business office sends a monthly budget report exported from the financial accounting system to all budget managers.

Interpretation without context: This budget report is from an accountant's viewpoint. It is not from the context that an academic administrator could easily understand. The report has numerous acronyms, column titles, terminology, and lines of code, which could be perceived to be largely unintelligible to non-accountants.

Interpretation with context: The budget contains a coversheet with a summary of revenue and expenditures with bolded and colored text along with a pie chart showing expenditures by category and remaining funds.

FIGURE 3.4 Context Scenario Three.

construct this frame of reference is key to the value of data. Data must become intimately tied to formalized context descriptions, a custom which this author believes to be by and large absent in the present-day university setting. Routine monthly reports, for example, should be accompanied by a background cover sheet (discussed in more detail later in this chapter), if one is to expect that the end user and recipient of the data report to make this tool integral in day-to-day performance. This should be made somewhat easier by the fact that many such reports now appear in email inboxes or are easily accessible online where "context popup boxes" could easily be created. Producers and users should think similarly of data and context. The awareness and effective management of context are key to unlocking the power of data, empowering users to make better decisions based upon data, and creating a lasting data culture.

Often a system chancellor and system governing board appoint a president for a campus, but they themselves have spent limited to no time at the institution getting to know the culture of the campus. It is often the culture of a campus that can make a president ineffective. Does a campus ever say, "Maybe we are wrong and not the president?" This president's strategy may be effective at another institution. It is important for data practitioners to provide the president with context so he or she can be successful (R. M. Zaccari, personal communication, February 17, 2017).

An attempt by data practitioners to gather contextual understanding can result in greater buy-in and success. When data and context are not used to initiate change, change does not experience long-term success. For example, at one institution, an incoming president changed an existing budget planning system in an effort to save positions from being eliminated. Some campus community members felt that the new president was not attempting to learn the path to its creation or examine its effectiveness. It was replaced by a system many considered far less effective, as evidenced by large sums of undesignated end-of-year funds that were used to fund existing positions and create infrastructure for the institution (i.e., new buildings). Reflecting on these types of activities, a former university president shared, "Sometimes you do not need to turn an institution upside down, just a new line of rhythm to transform the system slightly" (R. M. Zaccari, personal communication, February 17, 2017).

It would pay dividends to be able to view the data through the eyes of the various categories of consumers of the data, or campus constituents. Knight noted that although there may be concrete facts, "people understand what is going on and react based on who and where they are in the organization at any one time" (Knight, 2014, p. 111). Developing contextual intelligence requires placing the practitioner in the shoes of someone else who may be affected or impacted by the data while at the same time respecting their perspectives. Think about how data may affect the following constituents and groups, for example:

- Governing Board or Trustees
- President, Vice-Presidents, and Cabinet Officers
- Academic Administrators (Deans and department heads)
- Non-Academic Administrators (Directors and unit heads)
- Faculty Senate
- Staff Council
- Student Government Association
- Students, parents, and their families
- Community members and employers
- Legislators
- Accrediting agencies

PRACTICAL SUGGESTIONS AND GUIDANCE

This section provides readers with numerous strategies to integrate context into their work, particularly as they consume, produce, and interpret data for various constituencies.

Some individuals receiving data can very easily feel intimidated by it. One method to alleviate any potential discomfort is to create a background sheet for the data. This could be as simple as a list of questions, which you ask yourself before transmitting the final report. Often, presenters may provide context verbally in a meeting when distributing a report, but this relies on the listener retaining the context information. A background sheet on the report can help to institutionalize the context for a longer period of time than simply a one-hour meeting where the topic was discussed. The background sheet does not need to be as complex as a project charter, but it should be transparent so it can be used by those involved in the shared governance or collaborative decision-making process. Communication throughout the entire process is critical, and the background cover sheet is one tool to provide a sound introduction to the data or report. See Figure 3.5 for some sample questions for a background sheet.

There remains the question of who should weave these "baskets of context." These types of context descriptions should not be expected from those nearest the computers who push the print or send buttons. Of course, these employees should be included in meetings to arrive at relevant contextual information, but provosts, deans, and department heads as well as the intended recipients should be involved in examining each set of data with the idea in mind of establishing a set of the most pertinent variables influencing the numbers included in the data. After such an exercise, it should not be forgotten that these influences would likely not be static. Ideally, before each new report is generated, the context information should be reviewed for changes.

It is the opinion of this author that the expense of the additional time and resources used to set up and maintain such a system would be more than offset by the

Project name:

Expectations of requestor:

Expectations of originator:

How long has this report been produced?

Why is it necessary to produce this report?

What limitations impact the accuracy of the data provided in the report?

Which constituents will be positively impacted or negatively impacted by the distribution of the data?

Which individuals or groups need to review the information before it is generally released?

FIGURE 3.5 Sample Background Sheet.

increase in utility of the data, making it more easily understandable and therefore providing more responsive and successful systems throughout the campus. The nature of and purpose for all data reports arriving at the desk of a new employee and the attached background (or context) cover sheet must be a part of all new employee orientations. For example, if the data is generated by the business office, a business officer should sit with that employee to explain it in detail.

Practical Strategies for Gaining Institutional Context

- *Build relationships within the environment and be present in that environment.* Terenzini recommended, "purposefully seeking regular contact and conversation" (1999, p. 28) with administrators and non-administrators. A new president should make time to host listening sessions or open forums at the new institution.
- *Blend out of the current leadership circle and department/division to obtain context from other units.* Individuals will likely not randomly share, but when one attends such events, they will be more inclined to do so. One can easily stay on top of what is happening at the institution by following the campus calendar, reading the institution's news releases, and reading the strategic plans for the various divisions/units at the institution.
- *Move through multiple circles to conduct some preliminary research.* Have conversations about the institution's culture before implementing a major

directive. Ask around to colleagues, "Do you think this institution is ready for _____?" (Hill et al., 2017). Institutions can change but they must have the capacity to do so, which includes ability and willingness (Conner, 1992).

- *Identify individuals for a committee who can look holistically at the institution* (Hill et al., 2017). Consider a person who has served in several departments, committees, worked in numerous places throughout the campus over a period of years, or a person who has had experiences at different universities. Consider this scenario in Figure 3.6.

- *Select terms for initiatives which are positive and promote trust.* For example, the Achieving Strategic Balance Committee sounds more positive than the Program Reprioritization Committee (Hill et al., 2017). While selecting these terms, it is natural to seek some form of technological solution, however, some studies have indicated that individuals focus more on the technologies themselves rather than on how those technologies can be utilized (Marcella & Knox, 2004).

- *Benchmark against other institutions, display trends over time, and examine group differences to gain additional context* (Knight, 2017).

- *Join one or more of the numerous higher education professional networks.* Such networks provide opportunities for colleagues throughout the country to connect and learn from each other. Learning successes and mistakes from other institutions are keys to learning context. Not every idea is a good idea, and it is not always the most appropriate action to jump on the newest bandwagon if the organization's culture cannot handle it.

Declines in enrollments over the last five years have now reached a crisis level, and the institution has no option but to lay off personnel. The data to make decisions includes a list of faculty and staff by department with hire dates, salaries, and, if applicable, the number of credit hours taught.

Interpretation without context: Authorize lay-offs of the most recently hired across the institution until the required financial commitment can be met.

Interpretation with context: Examine lay-offs programmatically to ensure that a personnel lay-off does not impact the mission more negatively than the cost savings. For example, academic programs cannot operate adequately with only one full-time faculty member, and it would be more damaging to lay off a departmental secretary thereby leaving a department with no administrative support staff.

FIGURE 3.6 Context Scenario Four.

For example, not every institution is positioned to implement a competency-based education model, which is currently a growing interest area at many higher education institutions.

- *Read and learn about the history of the institution.* This may include published documents/histories or interviews (through recorded oral history projects or through retirees). Often, a project or initiative has been attempted previously, but is outside the frame of reference for the current decision makers. Learn more about the culture and history of the institution because the institution may now be capable of responding differently to the same situation.

- *Engage with new people entering the institution (or committee).* Knight (2017) recommended a simple sentence such as "If you ever want to know why (or how) something happened in the past, let me know and I will be glad to provide you with a short history." Do not act hesitantly or with frustration, when explaining something to a new colleague that has already been explained; perhaps that dean or department head was not there five, ten, or fifteen years ago.

- *Appoint an institutional context officer.* In any department, whether it is an institutional research office, a business office, or an academic affairs office, a context officer is needed. If funding were abundant, hiring an individual who would provide the context coversheet or background sheet for all communication could be a major step toward making released data useable by a greater number and used more efficiently by senior level administrators. If funding is not available, identify an individual with institutional history and who has the propensity to help piece everything together.

SUMMARY

Historically, universities have not made it easy for employees to understand and use data. Yet, administrators increasingly expect employees to act and plan based upon data. For too long, the specific uses of financial and other data reports have been left to the general expertise and experience of those for whom they are intended without specific orientation to them. Too often the results are suboptimal. It should be made clear that appropriate appreciation of and management of contextual information are missing pieces in our management puzzle. By improving access to context and merging it with the data, a communication rich process develops to ultimately create more viable decision-making.

DISCUSSION QUESTIONS

1. Identify a colleague or supervisor at your campus whom you believe possesses contextual intelligence. What characteristics does this person have and what actions has he or she done to indicate this intelligence?

2. Think about an impactful decision, either at the institutional or departmental level, which was made recently. What contextual factors were considered or not considered?

3. Select any two strategies from this chapter which discuss incorporating context and describe how you can apply them to your institution.

4. You have proposed to your supervisor the need to hire an institutional context officer. How do you justify this request? What are the knowledge, skills, and abilities you would look for in a candidate?

5. Your institution's governing board is responsible for over 20 institutions, and in order to maintain funding, it has been determined that the enrollment growth rate at the institution must meet or exceed 4%. However, the number of high school graduates is decreasing in the state and budgets are being reduced by 1%. Provide a reaction from the context of a faculty member, staff member, administrator, and student.

REFERENCES

Black, M. M. (2008). *Capital funding and institutional growth: A case study of regional state universities.* (Unpublished doctoral dissertation). Florida State University, Tallahassee, FL.

Bouckaert, G. (2013). Numbers in context: Applying Frege's Principles to public administration. In C. Pollitt (Ed.), *Context in public policy and management: The missing link?* (pp. 73–87). Northampton, MA: Edward Elgar Publishing.

Brown, K. R. (2016, November 7). A vision for Valdosta State University. Presentation.

Conner, D. R. (1992). *Managing at the speed of change: How resilient managers succeed and prosper where others fail.* New York: Villard Books.

Dey, A. K. (2001). Understanding and using context. *Personal and Ubiquitous Computing, 5*(1): 4–7.

Eimers, M. T., Ko, J. W., & Gardner, D. (2012). Practicing institutional research. In R. D. Howard, G. W. McLaughlin, & W. E. Knight (Eds.), *The handbook of institutional research* (pp. 40–56). San Francisco, CA: Jossey-Bass.

Hill, K., Loshbaugh, H., Grote, D., & Arcarese, C. (2017, June 2). Program prioritization for strategic resource (re)allocation, Association for Institutional Research Annual Forum, Washington, DC [PowerPoint slides].

Knight, W. E. (2014). *Leadership and management in institutional research: Enhancing personal and professional effectiveness*. Tallahassee, FL: Association for Institutional Research.

Knight, W. E. (2017, May 29). Leadership in institutional research and institutional effectiveness: Enhancing personal and professional effectiveness. Association for Institutional Research Annual Forum, Washington, DC [PowerPoint slides].

Lorentz, A. (2013, April). With big data, context is a big issue. *Wired*. Retrieved from www.wired.com/insights/2013/04/with-big-data-context-is-a-big-issue/.

Marcella, R. and Knox, K. (2004). Systems for the management of information in a university context: An investigation of user need. *Information Research, 9*(2) paper 172. Retrieved from http://InformationR.net/ir/9-2/paper172.html.

Swanson, J. & Rinehart, A. K. (2016). Data in context: using case studies to generate a common understanding of data in academic libraries. *The Journal of Academic Librarianship, 42*(1): 97–101. https://doi.org/10.1016/j.acalib.2015.11.005.

Terenzini, P. T. (1993). On the nature of institutional research and the knowledge and skills it requires. *Research in Higher Education, 34*(1): 1–10.

Terenzini, P. T. (1999). On the nature of institutional research and the knowledge and skills it requires. *New Directions for Institutional Research, 1999*(104): 21–29.

Terenzini, P. T. (2013). On the nature of institutional research revised: Plus ça change? *Research in Higher Education, 54*(2): 137–148.

Wiktionary. (2017). Context. Retrieved from https://en.wiktionary.org/wiki/context.

Part II

People, Leadership, and Relationships

Chapter 4

Identifying Decisions and Decision Makers that Drive Culture

Mihaela Tanasescu, Jeffrey L. Pellegrino, and Elna van Heerden

INTRODUCTION

Throughout this book, the value of data comes through in quality decision-making. In this chapter, we explore various decision-making roles in building and fostering a data culture. Foundational to this discussion is a belief that data is a "democratizer" in which all employees' effectiveness is maximized by participating in the culture in their day-to-day activity (Tunguz & Bien, 2016). Most faculty and staff who produce, report, and utilize data can thus be treated as decision makers. An important role in driving the culture is that of culture change leaders—a key decision maker, which will be explored as part of formal and informal opportunities.

IDENTIFYING DECISION MAKERS AND THEIR ROLES

No matter the role, four professional competencies exist to support a data culture that either need to be recruited or developed (see Figure 4.1). The competency of quantitative reasoning, which involves statistics and use of probability, factors into a person's ability to communicate about data with others and to answer questions credibly.

Another competency, practical knowledge of higher education or specifically the institution, is critical to understanding where data comes from, how to value it, and when to use it (for detailed discussion of the importance of institutional context, see Chapter 3). This would need to be developed strategically with the goal of establishing a perpetual culture of data. The third competency involves subject matter expertise where a person can be reflective on the actual practices under examination, providing a point of context to frame questions and translate ideas interprofessionally.

Being able to communicate effectively, the last competency, allows the other three to be effective, including the ability to receive, question, and provide

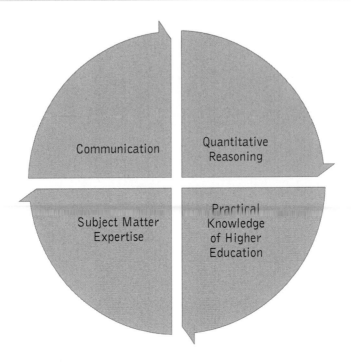

FIGURE 4.1 Professional Competencies Supporting a Data Culture.

feedback to colleagues. It also includes communicating data-derived decisions clearly and at various levels of understanding, while maintaining credibility. These four competencies do not exist necessarily in equal proportions for each person, but need balancing through interprofessional teams or professional development. As with other competencies, we want them manifested both in individuals and in teams, which, in addition to collaboration and goal alignment, will likely lead to stronger team outcomes.

Decision makers exist at all levels in every institution of higher education, on a continuum of "focus"—from a local (e.g., class content or room temperature) to global experiences (e.g., learning management system (LMS) or campus security). At the same time, decision makers span the continuum of "creativity"—from innovation to automation (see Figure 4.2). Recognizing that the continuums of focus and creativity intersect, situational data opportunities exist for the production and use of data. Such decisions affect various stakeholders (e.g., students, funders, community partners, corporate partners) in terms of number of people and quantity of data generated or used. These quadrants inform culture change leaders on motivations and implications for data use and the relationships to others.

Executive leaders need a strategy for identifying culture change leaders and data luddites to move an organization for which a stage approach to culture change

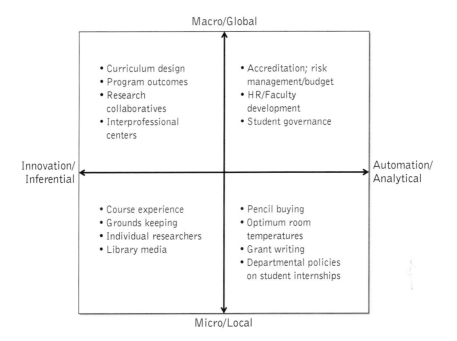

Macro/Global

- Curriculum design
- Program outcomes
- Research collaboratives
- Interprofessional centers

- Accreditation; risk management/budget
- HR/Faculty development
- Student governance

Innovation/Inferential

Automation/Analytical

- Course experience
- Grounds keeping
- Individual researchers
- Library media

- Pencil buying
- Optimum room temperatures
- Grant writing
- Departmental policies on student internships

Micro/Local

FIGURE 4.2 Data Use Quadrants. Creative Commons Attribution-NonCommercial 4.0 International—Pellegrino, 2017.

is appropriate. With everyone being a potential decision maker in how to identify, collect, or use data—a culture change leader needs to understand the importance of the stages of a cultural shift and to manage the change accordingly. If decision makers are unaware of the need to change or the organization has just had another major cultural change, the approach needs modification. For further discussion on organizational readiness, see Chapters 1 and 2. For a culture to value data, the cycle of data to wisdom (see Figure 4.3) must be internalized, but to achieve the adoption of this culture a social-behavioral approach is required. Two helpful explainers include the Transtheoretical Model (TTM) (Prochaska & DiClemente, 1983) for behavior change at the individual level and Social Diffusion theory (Rogers, 2003; Sahin, 2006) for behavioral change at the group level.

TTM brings theories of psychology, sociology, biology, and ecology together in a way that executive leaders may value the entirety of the organization and identify multiple strategies to move individuals. The stages include:

- *Pre-contemplation*: self-efficacy is at its lowest because there is no identified need to use data differently than current use.
- *Contemplation*: individuals see or feel a value, or are impacted using data differently, and participation with data or its use is recognized as an option.

45

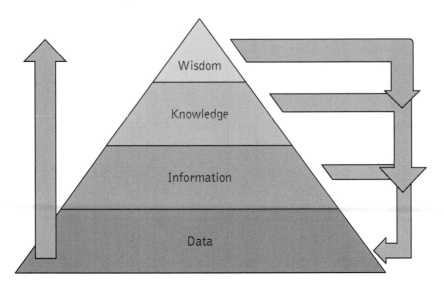

FIGURE 4.3 Data Cycle. Creative Commons Attribution-NonCommercial 4.0 International—Pellegrino, 2017.

- *Preparation*: learning about the options for participating in the idea or actual culture of data use. This may include formal learning or informal social learning, practical skill development, or be as simple as how to use institutional tools, like dashboards, and the value of departments of Institutional Research. Self-efficacy increases to a point of action.
- *Action*: individual practices are supported through the change period, allowing individuals to implement what they learned in their preparation stage. This stage allows individuals to find value from their change. If the person finds value in the change then she/he continues, if not she/he may "relapse" back into not participating.
- *Maintenance*: with practice, value, and ideally a system that supports a data culture the individual continues to make data-based decisions, until the contemplation for another change begins.

Moving between stages strategically requires attention at the individual level by leaders.

TTM focused on the individual, where Rogers' Social Diffusion Paradigm (2003) describes the main elements to infuse innovation culturally in stages: *Innovation perception* by another person, meaning someone must create something of value and be in a place where others can identify it. For example, enrollment services may create a useful database of potential students and their anticipated learning experiences, like service-learning, and others may use it to target marketing, while others use it to design co-curricular activities.

Individuals or another unit of adoption must perceive the innovation as an idea, practice, or object of value (Rogers, 1983). The characteristics of an innovation, as perceived by the members of a functional part, determine the innovation's rate of adoption. Five attributes of innovations that early adopters look for include: 1) relative advantage, 2) compatibility, 3) complexity, 4) trialability, and 5) observability. Each attribute may be engineered or come naturally to the innovation but all are helpful to the culture change leader.

Any innovative cultural data use will not diffuse into the culture unless it is *communicated* through valued channels. Most individuals evaluate an innovation not based on scientific research but through the subjective evaluations of near-peers who have previously adopted the innovation. This communication allows individuals a means to contemplate their role in a culture of data, as discussed previously in the TTM. Communication and contemplation also need *time to mimic and adopt innovations.* Transfer of the innovation may seem slow to cultural change leaders, but this time period allows for kinks and challenges to be resolved in the changing culture. Adoption becomes faster once the innovation becomes easier for others to implement. Culture change leaders recognize time as an important element in the innovation-decision process and build it into strategic planning.

Rogers cautions that studying the innovation process in organizational settings represents a shift from the classical diffusion model in important ways. Innovation at the organizational level might not be a fixed or static element, but rather an adaptable idea that can be redefined leading to reinventions. Reinvention could and should be the fabric of college/university life to meet individual and social needs inside and outside of our work. Empowering individuals to recognize themselves as a decision maker is a start to changing the culture. Leaders need to establish ways for individuals to appropriately access data, move data forward, produce information, and be a literate receiver of information or evidence-based decisions.

Establishing expectations based on types of data (e.g., student level, course, program, department, institution) cannot be only on the automation end of the creativity continuum, if innovativeness is to be part of the institutional culture. Reflecting on data and creating linkages to the organization and stakeholders at all levels affects higher-level institutional outcomes. In addition, valuing "business" and "academic" data equally will demonstrate mission and help socially diffuse evidence-based practices.

VALUING AND LEGITIMIZING DATA USE IN DECISION-MAKING

Culture change leaders and decision makers should understand the intent of the use of data, trust the sources and quality of the data, and accept the impact of evidence-based decision-making to foster change. Another critical consideration is trust between leaders and other decision makers around data sources, its validity, reliability, and intent to socialize and drive a data culture. These critical considerations inform the progression toward more advanced use of data (see Figure 4.3).

Leaders and other decision makers, who understand the intent of the data (at multiple levels in their organizations), are in positions to demonstrate the value of adopting a data culture and the potential impact of evidence-based decision-making. An example of clear communication of the intent of data is for "higher education to achieve the values of equity, transparency and quality it espouses; and ensure that all students graduate in a timely fashion with the competencies they need to be active and productive citizens" (Maki & Kuh, 2017, Foreword).

Also, culture change leaders have opportunities to encourage and engage faculty and staff to experience data in support of the unique value and characteristics of the institution. "Assessment results should tell an important, coherent, interesting story" of an institution (Suskie, 2009, p. 280). The adoption of a data culture and bringing people into the decision-making role across institutions of higher education requires an alignment of values.

Environmental competition and compliance imperatives shaped much of the progress toward a data-informed approach in higher education in long and short terms. For example, emphasis on accountability plays a major role in the advanced data orientation of private for-profit institutions. Such institutions must gather, report, and improve on metrics that are not required for degree programs offered in public and private non-profit institutions: gainful employment debt reporting and disclosures, additional data for state authorization, and financial aid for the 90–10 rule. An exclusive dependence on tuition and fee revenue further strengthens the need for data. Similarly, an emphasis on student outcomes forces a data culture in community colleges (Norris & Baer, 2012). In the "Achieving the Dream" initiative that began in 2004, the Lumina Foundation supported the academic success of community college students by making data a central part of the culture. While results were mixed, the experience provided data, information, knowledge, and wisdom for future interventions. Most importantly, it underscored the value for fundamental organizational change and teamwork in utilizing data for student success (Bailey, Smith Jaggars, & Jenkins, 2015).

Valuing data use as part of the institution in explicit or implicit manners and supporting it with actions, resources, and follow-up helps align the culture for all participants (Norris & Baer, 2012). Those within the culture see and benefit from value commitment in true resources like equipping the organization with data access and professionally developing staff and faculty to make decisions. Strategic plans may include goals and initiatives that pertain to the data systems and the related investment. In addition to values, mission, and goals, quality assurance processes are likely to influence the adoption of a data culture (Hora, Bouwma-Gearhart, & Park, 2014). As such, policies and practices will routinize using analytics, data utilization, and a student success orientation.

TRUST IN THE INTEGRITY OF THE DATA

Culture change leaders and decision makers who communicate the intent of data on the focus continuum also need to trust the integrity of the data from local sources to legitimize its use. This is because evidence does not speak for itself but rather "it [data] requires interpretation, integration, and reflection in the search for holistic understanding and implications for action" moving from data to information to knowledge (Kuh et al., 2015, pp. 2–3). Trust, starting with institutional motives that foster data-informed decision-making may be limited in a culture of reporting and compliance in part because there are motivations other than the pursuit of knowledge and making effective decisions. Paralleling the trust concern for reporting-based cultures is what Kuh et al. (2015) described as "initiative fatigue" (p. 5) that develops when campuses are swamped by the competing demands of assessment for compliance, sometimes without a vision for improvement and follow-up. To prevent this, culture change leaders and decision makers can identify overlapping demands and explain nuances that will lead to performance enhancement. Institutions can establish multiple opportunities to use the same data, for example, student outcomes, by promoting a culture of assessment at institutional, program, and course levels.

If culture change leaders or decision makers miss creating the value and intent of the data, trust in the data process, or accepting the impact of decisions, the institution will not inherently fail. But, the culture of data will not exist because it will not make sense to the stakeholders in the organization. The four professional competencies that support a data culture (quantitative reasoning, practical knowledge of higher education or specifically the institution, subject matter expertise, and effective communication) will not, on their own, create a culture of data.

BRINGING PEOPLE INTO THE ROLE OF DECISION-MAKING

Historically, higher education institutions have been generating and reporting data, rather than routinely applying results to improve outcomes (Blaich & Wise, 2010). More recently, a migration from a "culture of reporting" to a "culture of evidence" is observed, where analytics provide actionable intelligence that provoke actions and interventions, such as supporting at-risk students (Norris & Baer, 2012). Moving from evidence to a "culture of performance," where faculty and staff actions optimize student and institutional success, needs orchestration and measurement, with a focus on continuously improving results.

Institutions must determine the needed knowledge and skills to progress through the stages of reporting, evidence, and performance. Areas of attention for culture change leaders should include the perceived lack of time, lack of expertise, and poor data quality as limiting factors of data use. Assessment cycles, program reviews, and accreditation requirements are generally an impetus for data use, but they may also foster a compliance, "check the box" approach. Recognizing the influence of faculty and staff structures and the centralized or decentralized nature of individual institutions will also need accounting for by culture change leaders.

TRAINING, DEVELOPMENT, AND RECOGNITION

As institutional needs span the focus and creativity continuums, training and development are necessary for specific roles as well as to develop an institutional understanding of the value of data. In general, a data culture is well served by hiring employees who value data and curiosity, and who, regardless of experience, rely less on gut instincts and anecdotes and more on evidence, along with the competencies mentioned above. Nonetheless, if we follow the example of advanced corporate entities that demonstrate data-informed decision-making and success, they tend to excel not just in hiring highly qualified talent, but also at professional development (Maynard, n.d.). Institutions of higher education should seek to maximize the effect of both its hiring selection and its professional development, while focusing on its data priorities. Valuing the unique knowledge and skill of each faculty and staff member will foster the self-actualization of individual contributors as decision makers in a data democracy. At the same time, teams accomplish outcomes through the complementary contribution of individuals, collaboration, and goal alignment. Professional development should seek to address individual, as well as group contributions. There should be a standard set of data knowledge and skills in which the entire organization will be versed, an advanced specialization for each job category, and a valuing of individual contributions, keeping in mind that teams are flexible and we want long-term success.

The advent of big data analytics may pose a challenge in terms of the kinds of data faculty and staff would monitor, use, and affect, but the Data Use Quadrants (Figure 4.2) illustrate a connection between users and data of any size. "Small data" gathered in the classroom, and the use of individual and qualitative approaches may add important components to the big picture and may help solve and answer many questions. The availability of experts in each phase of the data cycle is an important factor for overall cultural development. This may include colleagues who routinely discuss discipline-based educational research, centers of excellence, and focused projects (Hora et al., 2014).

An issue that arises frequently and that may impede data use is the inadequate understanding of variables and indicators of success. Training on data dictionaries and on ways to find data, produce specific reports, and act based on them will be key in developing self-reliance. Furthermore, it will be essential to integrate data utilization in standard operation procedures. Levels of proficiency will ultimately still vary at the individual level, but the key outcomes and performance indicators will be understood by all. The institution will also have to decide the levels of freedom for reviewing and acting on data. Moderate levels of freedom and formal avenues for experimentation are shown to be conducive to success in the corporate environment (Maynard, n.d.).

Creating multiple opportunities to develop quantitative reasoning skills across the organization engenders a spirit of "democratizing of data" across individual teams or stakeholders. Although units, like advising, registrar's office, and marketing can develop and offer training, there is practical benefit for making experiences interprofessional.

Data integration into daily work across the institution must also be considered in the job expectations, supervision, and reward of employees. Rewarding faculty and staff for consistently utilizing data and for identifying opportunities through data can be done publicly or through pay structures. Culture change leaders may find value in more public displays of rewards, while the long-term goal is for it to be done in an ongoing manner through institutionalized reward programs.

DECISION-MAKING MISTAKES

Mistakes can be grouped into two categories: one, making poor decisions because of the data process; and two, creating poor data processes. As described above, the four professional competencies to foster a data culture must be in balance to have a solid foundation to limit mistakes. Culture change leaders need to recruit for, professionally develop, assess, and reward based on these competencies to limit mistakes in creating and interpreting data.

Although one does not set out to create a poor data process, some characteristics should be avoided or worked out of a data culture:

- *"Data hogging."* For even the best reasons, data hogging limits the collaborative culture needed to make the most use of that data. Certain individuals may assume that they are the only ones who have the right experience to interpret data.
- *Denial of data.* Across the continuum of creativity, mistakes can be made by dismissing the data before decisions are made.

51

- *Assuming data isn't biased or presented without bias.* Advancing the data culture will support a trustworthiness of data, as participants become more aware of context and influences.
- *Lack of trust in the value and intent of data.* For example, if change leaders or decision makers don't have the practical knowledge of their institution or department and are not able to communicate evidence-based decisions effectively, it could impact the perceived value or intent of the data.
- *Uncoordinated decision-making.* This is often due to uncoordinated data and lack of collaboration among departments.
- *Presenting an incomplete picture.* Communicating outcomes needs to be based on key performance indicators that assess different dimensions of success. Drawing conclusions and making decisions considering a variety of outcomes may be based on an inaccurate picture of where the institution is in achieving its targets. For example, various groups of students may have very different retention behaviors on a short-term versus a longer-term basis, so the institution must consider a set of relevant outcomes. All outcome areas are generally described by more than one indicator. Determining the battery of indicators to be utilized for various types of decisions will generally prevent an incomplete picture and deciding too early or too late.
- *Presence of an isolationist culture.* Such cultures limit sharing data from and to outside stakeholders. External data may be important to the culture or even the existence of an institution, for example, data on the socioeconomic and demographic characteristics of potential students and faculty, data on employers, and on higher education in general. Conversely, sharing data externally, more like in health care and business, can further the institutional agenda.
- *Distancing faculty from institutional data.* Faculty members' socialization to institutional data will nurture their use of data in academic processes (e.g., courses or research).

PRACTICAL SUGGESTIONS AND GUIDANCE

Promoting Data Use

To infuse innovations with or by data, cultural channels by which the innovation or awareness of its existence is communicated need to be fostered organically and by change leaders. Not all channels are equal. For example, mention of a data innovation in a daily newsletter would not have the same value as a special note from the president or special funding. Use of mass media (e.g., mass email, websites) provides an effective means to creating awareness-knowledge of innovations, whereas interpersonal channels may be more effective in forming, and in changing, attitudes toward a new idea, and thus indirectly influencing the decision to adopt or reject a new idea. Seeking stakeholder input in the development and the continuous improvement of reports and dashboards and other channels promotes the growth and diffusion of a data culture.

In our experience, case studies of how data use yielded positive results can invite or inspire others. External examples will be instructive in some ways, but there is always the question of how applicable approaches are in a different institution. Hence, utilizing internal modeling of new data behavior will likely be more effective in promoting and reinforcing a data culture.

Other practical suggestions include:

- *Speed dating through data.* An experience where different collectors of data share data sets to allow new personnel to know what is collected and why, which might happen at new employee orientations or mid-level manager workshops; practically new people rotate in small groups or individuals to each "data manager" for 8 minutes, which gives a sense of data culture and sharing, knowing the system, knowing new people's interests, as well as networking.
- *Show & Tell.* A 15–30-minute conference style presentation or *Gallery walk* (10–20-minute mini-presentation based on posters or visuals spread throughout a meeting space) with the goal to present where "you" are in the data to wisdom continuum and the story of how you arrived and where you need to go, then to collect input from the audience. This forces individuals or groups to organize their thoughts for peer review and then socializes the idea of feedback for growth.
- *Including data as part of regular meeting agendas.* Report on data collection, or decisions based on data as part of standing meetings or regular gatherings across the institution. These regular activities will enable participants to begin to understand the impact of data, trust sources of data, and create opportunities to embed data in decision-making. Similarly, exploring what went wrong when poor outcomes are recorded needs to rely on data. The academic culture should also encourage faculty members to assess their students' learning outcomes and share that information with others in a way that builds on success.

Data Accessibility

Embracing the value of a data culture means in part enhanced data accessibility for all members of the culture (Tunguz & Bien, 2016).

- *Communicate key data.* Periodic central communication of key metrics and information sessions by institutional research, assessment, analytics, and business intelligence are macro/global examples of alignment and transparency.

53

■ *Create data dashboards.* Dashboards provide a practical way of making data broadly available for individuals across the institution. They focus on the metrics deemed most useful and aligned with the mission. They need to be designed with clarity and simplicity. Socially, they provide a non-intimidating way to interact with the data, and they may allow for exploration and innovation. The design of dashboards must include broad stakeholder input and further opportunity for refinement. Committees and teams can come up with new ideas and articulate additional data needs.

Hiring, Developing, and Rewarding for a Data-Driven Culture

Characteristics that are supportive of creating a data culture can be assessed in prospective hires.

■ *Hire for data competency.* Although candidates may not have formal data user titles, human resources departments may support the development of job descriptions that capture the essence of data competencies being sought. Evidence might be presented in portfolios, project work, or administrative roles candidates may have served in. For some roles, it might be enough to seek a demonstrated curiosity and a desire for solid decision-making.

■ *Evaluate and reward data use.* Utilizing data, once made an explicit part of job responsibilities, can be evaluated and perhaps more importantly, be rewarded. Tying awards and recognition for those contributing to a data culture in exceptional ways, serves institutional goals and strategic imperatives. Traditionally siloed, institutions of higher education have many opportunities to create a social system or set of interrelated units engaged in joint problem-solving to accomplish a common goal that should also be celebrated. Teaching cooperation and team-building interdepartmentally is also recommended, so that decisions are made with the overall institutional needs in mind.

■ *Host a "Data Day."* For cultures transitioning to usi ng data on a normal basis, offering a "Data Day" once a semester or quarter can accomplish this. "Digging into Data Day" (D3) or "Data Deciphering Day" (D3) can be celebrations of sorts when facilitated toward cultural norms or values. An associate dean who started them in one of our colleges kept the format loose between Data Days, allowing for the full cycle of data to be used over time. Benefits of Data Day included recognition of individuals for quality work and setting the environment for the diffusion of data into the culture. Data Days might consist of a multiple hour experience, scheduled once or twice per semester. Formats might include two or three presentations of different data or modeling a new technique to analyze data, or even working with a specific data set toward theory or decision-making.

SUMMARY

Developing an effective data culture begins with communicating its essential value for student outcomes and institutional success. In an advanced data culture, a majority of faculty and staff act as decision makers on a continuum of magnitude of impact and innovation. Models of behavior change and diffusion of innovation help to conceptualize the leadership approach to foster a progression toward advanced levels of the culture performance. Valuing data-based decision-making, ensuring trust, providing easy data access, developing staff and employees for local use and global understanding of metrics, as well as rewarding and communicating success of data-based approaches will support rigorous decision-making and the achievement of desired outcomes.

DISCUSSION QUESTIONS

1. Using the Creativity and Focus continuums, identify examples in your institution of how data is vertically integrated along the focus continuum and horizontally integrated on the creativity continuum.

2. Choose a practical suggestion that resonates to your institutional need and then create a plan on who to invite and why. Discuss how these innovators might help diffuse the use of data into the culture of the institution based on Rogers' work.

3. Review your institution's mission, vision, values, and strategic plan. How is a data culture represented? Is it an implicit or an explicit representation? Is the institution well prepared to achieve its goals from a data culture perspective?

4. Consider the data needs of various departments in your institution. What types of training and development can lead to the further development of a data culture? Does it vary by role? What would make the most difference in outcomes?

5. Consider the ways in which decision makers in organizations view data and communicate the use of data in organizational cultures. How could understanding data, trust, and respecting the impact of data affect an institution's data culture?

6. Consider various groups of stakeholders within the institution. What are the barriers to data utilization for decision-making? Do they have access to the data they need? Do they have the competencies necessary to systematically use data in day-to-day decisions?

7. Consider accreditation and compliance reporting in your institution. Is it conducive to a data culture? Why or why not? How can it be effectively used to foster a data culture?

REFERENCES

Bailey, T. R., Smith Jaggars, S., & Jenkins, D. (2015). *Redesigning America's community colleges: A clearer path to student success*. Cambridge, MA : Harvard University Press.

Blaich, C. F. & Wise, K. S. (2010). Moving from assessment to institutional improvement. *New Directions for Institutional Research*, 67–78.

Hora, M. T., Bouwma-Gearhart, J., & Park, H. J. (2014). *Exploring data-driven decision-making in the field: How faculty use data and other forms of information to guide instructional decision-making. WCER Working Paper No. 2014–3*. Madison, WI: Wisconsin Center for Education Research.

Kuh, G. D., Ikenberry, S. O., Jankowski, N. A., Cain, T. R., Ewell, P. T., Hutchings, P., & Kinzie, J. (2015). *Using evidence of student learning to improve higher education*. San Francisco, CA: Jossey-Bass.

Maki, P. & Kuh, G. D. (2017). *Real-Time student assessment: Meeting the imperative for improved time to degree, closing the opportunity gap, and assuring student competencies for 21st century needs*. Sterling, VA: Stylus.

Maynard, S. (n.d.). *Data and Analytics Impact Index 2015: Don't forget the human element of analytics*. Jersey City, NJ. Retrieved from www.ey.com/Publication/vwLUAssets/EY-Forbes-Insights-Data-and-Analytics-Impact-Index-2015/$FILE/EY-Forbes-Insights-Data-and-Analytics-Impact-Index-2015.pdf.

Norris, D. M. & Baer, L. (2012). Building organizational capacity for analytics. *Proceedings of the 2nd International Conference Learning Analytics & Knowledge*. Louisville, CO: EDUCAUSE. Retrieved from www.educause.edu/ir/library/pdf/PUB 9012.pdf.

Prochaska, J. O. & DiClemente, C. C. (1983). Stages and processes of self-change of smoking: Toward an integrative model of change. *Journal of Consulting and Clinical Psychology, 51*(3): 390–395.

Rogers, E. M. (1983). *Diffusion of innovations*. New York: Free Press; London: Collier Macmillan.

Rogers, E. M. (2003). *Diffusion of innovations*. New York: Free Press.

Sahin, I. (2006). Detailed review of Rogers' Diffusion of Innovations Theory and Educational Technology-Related Studies based on Rogers' Theory. *The Turkish Online Journal of Educational Technology—TOJET April, 5*(3), 1303–6521. Retrieved from http://tojet.net/articles/v5i2/523.pdf.

Suskie, L. A. (2009). *Assessing student learning: A common sense guide*. San Francisco, CA : Jossey-Bass.

Tunguz, T. & Bien, F. (2016). *Winning with data: Transform your culture, empower your people, and shape the future*. Hoboken, NJ: John Wiley & Sons.

Chapter 5

Changing Questions Asked

Lori Williams

INTRODUCTION

Over one hundred years ago, in a book titled *How We Think* (1910/1997), John Dewey shared his views on thinking, and specifically about thinking in the context of learning and education. In describing the difficulty he saw that teachers and administrators faced, amid a multiplicity of tasks, materials, disciplines, and principles upon which to draw in their work, Dewey called upon learners and educators themselves to cultivate a scientific "attitude of mind" or "habit of thought" that requires conscious attention to retraining one's own thinking processes (1910/1997).

The questions that leaders in higher education ask of themselves, their administrators, faculty, institutional research staff, and other internal and external stakeholders are a function of what and how they think about their purposes and goals. Much as Dewey did, this chapter invites educators to become consciously aware of how they think and to use that awareness to consider how their thinking influences the questions they ask, as they both specify the types of data they choose to collect and the ways they analyze those data. Understanding one's own thinking about data and the use of data is considered here in the context of the factors that influence current thinking, the issues and challenges with current thinking, new approaches to thinking differently, and practical suggestions for applying these new approaches.

For leaders to consciously influence the creation of an effective and positive data culture, they must first become aware of their thinking and how their thinking has been influenced, consciously reframe their thinking, test this new thinking, and ask new data questions that may potentially implement changes. Figure 5.1 offers a framework for understanding and implementing a shift in thinking that is explored in more detail in the following sections.

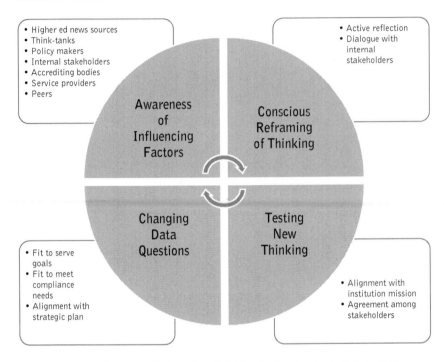

- Higher ed news sources
- Think-tanks
- Policy makers
- Internal stakeholders
- Accrediting bodies
- Service providers
- Peers

- Active reflection
- Dialogue with internal stakeholders

Awareness of Influencing Factors

Conscious Reframing of Thinking

Changing Data Questions

Testing New Thinking

- Fit to serve goals
- Fit to meet compliance needs
- Alignment with strategic plan

- Alignment with institution mission
- Agreement among stakeholders

FIGURE 5.1 The Process of Changing Thinking in the Context of Data Culture Creation.

FACTORS THAT INFLUENCE CURRENT THINKING

A multitude of factors influences the current thinking of higher education leaders including chancellors, presidents, provosts, deans, and chairs, which in turn shapes the culture of data use at their institutions. These factors include, but are not limited to, the beliefs and behaviors of higher education news organizations and think-tanks, peers and competitors, accrediting bodies, policymakers at the state and federal levels, and the proliferation of third-party providers who offer services to collect and report on institution data. Academic leaders also call upon each other, their deans and chairs, faculty governance bodies, and members of their boards of trustees to help shape their thinking.

Many higher education leaders begin their days by reading the news about their peers in *The Chronicle of Higher Education* and *Inside Higher Ed* in their daily email messages. These news stories reflect the current thinking of the leaders and policymakers about which they report, and the reactions of faculty, staff, students, and the general public to these news items. Writers and editors of their news outlets, however neutral and unbiased they strive to be, also influence the current thinking of higher education leaders. Higher education professional associations, organizations, and think-tanks write reports and white papers that influence thinking, and sponsor conferences at which leaders share their views.

In the context of developing new academic programs and in the program reviews of existing programs, leaders look to their peers and competitors to benchmark and compare many aspects of their planned and existing programs. Academic leaders want their programs to be comparable, competitive, marketable, and appropriate in content and outcomes. They review website descriptions of their peers' programs and the Integrated Postsecondary Education Data System (IPEDS) for these data, and if resources are available, they may hire outside firms like Eduventures to conduct competitor research for them.

Federal and state regulatory bodies require higher education institutions to collect and report data on multiple aspects of a college or university including enrollment, graduation and retention rates, demographic and socio-economic characteristics of students, and job placement rates (National Center for Education Statistics). The types of data these regulatory bodies require are a function of the beliefs and attitudes of the people who make up those organizations. Leaders respond to these data requests in order to comply with regulations, but also to indirectly respond to questions asked in the context of what and how state and federal government agencies are thinking about the purposes and goals of higher education.

One example of a shift in higher education thinking is the move from questions about who goes to college, to questions about who graduates from college. Beginning in the late 1950s, when the National Defense Education Act emphasized increasing access to higher education, the questions and thinking had to do with who goes to college. Later in the 1990s, the questions shifted to who graduates (Tinto, 2004), producing a greater focus and attention on graduation and retention rates, as opposed to admissions policies and access to higher education. Today the questions have shifted toward asking what jobs graduates obtain and how much money they make in those jobs.

The expectations that organizations, think-tanks, and foundations set also influence the larger higher education culture in which leaders work. These include think-tanks like New America, the Brookings Institution, and the Heritage Foundation, foundations like the Lumina Foundation, and the Bill & Melinda Gates Foundation, as well as professional organizations like the American Council on Education, the American Association of Universities and Colleges, the American Association of University Professors, and the Council on Higher Education Accreditation. The leaders of these and other organizations like them seek to influence the thinking not only of higher education institutions, but also of policy makers and members of the general public.

Each of these organizations begins with particular values and accompanying agendas and seek to influence higher education culture. Think-tanks, for example, tend to represent political or interest group agendas. The Heritage Foundation has sought to influence the United States Department of Education in the interest of decentralization of decision-making and improving opportunity for innovation (Hall & Reim, 2017). New America describes itself as a non-partisan organization that provides policy analysis, and with respect to higher education, in support of expanding opportunity for historically disadvantaged populations (Ekowo & Palmer, 2016). The Lumina Foundation promotes educational attainment beyond high school and invites its website visitors to consider "how we can increase levels of educational attainment equitably, through the use of quality data to improve student performance, identify problems, measure progress toward the goal and inform policy and decision-making at all levels" (Lumina Foundation, n.d.). These types of organizations influence higher education data culture through sponsoring research, publishing white papers, and lobbying policy makers, for just a few examples.

Accrediting bodies also influence thinking about data through the requirements they set for collecting and reporting these data. Regional accreditors, for example, require colleges and universities to report data on a regular basis about the number of programs they offer, the numbers of students enrolled, student demographic information, and student learning achievement, including measures of graduation and retention rates (WASC Senior College and University Commission, 2013). The United States Department of Education's National Center for Education Statistics (NCES) requires all institutions that participate in federal financial aid programs to publicly report on data regarding their programs, students, and staff. The consequences of not reporting these data to government agencies and accreditors are serious and potentially affect the very viability of colleges and universities.

The specific kinds of data required of accreditors and government agencies also influences thinking. Asking for data on the race, ethnicity, and gender of staff by the NCES through IPEDS requirements sets expectations for institutions about the fairness of serving as an equal opportunity employer as well as expectations from accreditors about the importance of a diverse staff serving the needs of a diverse student body.

To assist in compliance with federal and state regulations as well as accreditation standards, a number of service providers have established themselves to help colleges and universities collect and analyze data. These third-party companies offer institutions services to collect, store, manage, and analyze data that might otherwise be the purview of marketing, enrollment management, or institutional research departments. These services can be helpful to institutions who are new to these uses for data, or whose uses for data management have outgrown their internal staff's capacity. The providers have set expectations for institutions' ability to collect and analyze large data sets to learn more about how to improve learning, student retention, and graduation rates.

Helix Education, for example, an outsourced program management (OPM) company, assists institutions in collecting data not only to assist in complying with these regulatory requirements, but also to make the most of tuition revenue through services that maximize student initial enrollment and persistence, since students who persist improve the financial standing of the institution (Helix Education, 2017). Like other OPMs, Helix invites institutions to think of their student time with the college or university in the way businesses view their customers in the context of a "lifecycle" of engagement with the institution, from pre-enrollment through graduation, collecting data about student satisfaction, learning, and persistence. At each stage of the student lifecycle, depending upon the data about each student, institutions are expected to engage in interventions, sometimes designed or suggested by the OPMs, to improve satisfaction, learning, and persistence (Fong & Kovar, 2016). This practice of student lifestyle mapping has now gained traction as a best practice to help administrators think from the point of view of students, expanding their own thinking as it pertains to the journey that a student takes. These services and recommended practices may also change administrators' thinking through analyzing the data collected to glean important clues about the reasons for student success and persistence.

The combined expectations of accreditors, policymakers, and regulatory bodies that institutions will collect and analyze data with the goal of maximizing student learning and persistence is pushing educators to think more like business leaders. Some leaders may see a loftier purpose for themselves as academic administrators, and express disdain for reducing their roles in the adult development of their students to customer transactions. Yet recognizing a hierarchy of needs for students is important, understanding that student persistence is dependent on having their basic needs met first, before they can attain the institutions' mission for students' higher order achievements.

ISSUES AND CHALLENGES WITH CURRENT THINKING

Leaders in higher education are faced with issues and challenges related to data. Some of these challenges lie with external stakeholders asking for data to answer questions that speak to their underlying thinking and assumptions, and some issues come from internal sources. In both cases, leaders may or may not intentionally take a step back and reflect on their own thinking about these uses of data and the questions they ask or attempt to answer.

One challenge with current thinking as it pertains to external stakeholders, whether examined willfully or not, includes the need to comply with government and accreditation bodies' requirements. Recognizing the practical needs for collecting, reporting, and analyzing data to comply with state and federal regulatory and accreditation requirements does not necessarily threaten the individual and collective autonomy of thinking about data at academic institutions. Unconsciously asking questions and having one's thinking defined solely by others, whether regulatory bodies, other external stakeholders, faculty and deans, or board members, especially if unconsciously, is not constructive. Weighing the differing views of others and becoming consciously aware of the influence over one's own thinking will bring clarity and align thinking with purpose, especially in the context of the unique mission and vision of an institution.

One way to begin to become aware of the implicit or explicit questions external stakeholders ask is to consider the reports required of colleges and universities by government and accrediting bodies. Common requests of institutions for data include retention rates, graduation rates, and student demographic statistics. Producing these data presumably provides a response to questions about the value and quality of the education that students of differing backgrounds and experiences receive at this institution.

Some, however, have begun to challenge the assumptions that underlie these types of questions and data requests. Massy (2011), for example, suggests that institutions measure the value of higher education in terms of a ratio of outputs as measured against inputs so that they may consider the potential waste of resources used formerly not considered in measuring persistence and graduation. Another example of changing the questions in higher education data culture with respect to measuring outputs against inputs comes in the context of measuring graduation rates at the WASC Senior University and College Commission (WSCUC) through the implementation of its Graduation Rate Dashboard (GRD). The GRD automatically calculates completion measures for its member institutions in two ways, both based on a ratio of inputs to outputs. The first is the Unit Redemption Rate, which measures the units, or credits that are completed that count for a degree against the total number of units associated with the courses in which students enroll. The second is the Absolute Graduation Rate, which measures the ratio of students who enroll against those who eventually graduate. These measures and the questions they attempt to answer, differ from traditional measures like the IPEDS graduation rate requirements, since IPEDS measures assume all college students are cohort-based, first-time, full-time students, whereas these WSCUC-developed measures do not. These WSCUC measures of completion assume different questions about the nature of student behavior and their previous academic experiences.

Issues with thinking about data and its usage are not limited to those coming from external stakeholders, but also from internal sources, and present challenges to higher education leaders as well. Some of the reasons for these issues with thinking are discussed next in the context of cognitive biases.

NEW APPROACHES TO THINKING DIFFERENTLY

To begin to think differently, one must first develop awareness of one's own thinking processes. There are many ways to go about developing this awareness and two approaches are considered here, drawing on the research of Langer (1989) and Kahneman (2011). Langer (1989) describes the process of becoming more mindful of the ways in which one creates categories of types of thoughts, such that one uncovers the ways in which people somewhat automatically categorize their thoughts. She champions a particular understanding of "mindfulness," in the context of the need to challenge one's existing categories and intentionally create new categories to free up mental energy, creativity, and effectiveness. In this way, "mindfulness leads to feelings of control, greater freedom of action, and less burnout" (Langer, 1989, p. 202).

Langer also cautions against the misguided assumption that decision-making is solely a function of collecting data, since it is people who make decisions after they interpret and analyze data, and people bring limitations of thought and experience, which she argues must be broadened. One solution to this challenge that Langer offers is simply changing one's context. Changing context, literally or figuratively, can lead to new energy to combat fatigue and a fresh perspective. Even through just imagining the broad ideas and viewpoints of outsiders or other stakeholders, one can find a new openness to multiple, previously unconsidered perspectives (Langer 1989).

Like Langer, Kahneman (2011) suggests becoming more aware of one's thinking in order to change it. His approach begins with an understanding of his conception of two systems of mind that work together. The first is what Kahneman calls "System 1" in which initial impressions and feelings result in "thinking fast," whereas "System 2" requires more mental effort and produces conscious reasoning. When these two systems do not work well together, the outcome can involve a number of cognitive biases that can have a negative impact on decision-making. Becoming more aware of these two systems of thinking, and how they may result in biases can help individuals avoid pitfalls in thinking.

Consider three common biases in the context of data culture in higher education institutions: anchoring bias, confirmation bias, and outcome bias. Anchoring bias involves the over reliance on the value of the first data point considered, forming an attachment to that value without accurately estimating the range within which that data point might exist. The impact of this form of bias is that an unhelpful initial number absurdly influences people's judgments (Kahneman, 2011). In the context of higher education data culture, for example, one might begin an exploration of the first year retention rate of a cohort of students by comparing that rate with the previous year's rate. Assumptions may be made about the improvement or decline of that rate, based solely on the anchoring effect of the previous year's rate. The challenge for educators may be

63

compounded by the lack of previous years' data, especially in situations in which there are few institutional research personnel or a new program has been launched without comparable data.

Confirmation bias is the tendency to attend only to the data that confirms one's preconceptions. Although most higher education leaders hold PhDs and their training includes expectations to test hypotheses by trying to disprove them, Kahneman (2011) suggests that often the opposite tendency is employed. This form of bias strikes at the heart of the need to change the questions asked in the context of shifting into a more effective data culture. One must ask new and uncomfortable questions and be open-minded enough to look squarely at data that refute one's initial preconceived notions.

A third form of bias discussed by Kahneman (2011) is outcome bias. Here one determines the value of a decision based on the outcome of that decision rather than questioning how one came to the decision, often overlooking the sheer randomness of that outcome. Our minds are uncomfortable with not knowing, so we have a tendency to see patterns in randomness that are not supported by sufficient evidence. This particular form of bias can lead to erroneous conclusions, for example, in the context of designing and testing interventions intended to improve persistence and retention. It is very difficult to isolate the variables that may have an impact on persistence and so if the results of the test show improved persistence in the experimental group, researchers are likely to attribute the improvement to the intervention when the results may be completely random.

PRACTICAL SUGGESTIONS AND GUIDANCE

Faculty and academic leaders ask their students to cultivate a spirit of openness to new ideas in order to develop critical thinking skills. To shift thinking, leaders must similarly foster their own attitude of broad and expansive possibility.

Given what we know about the limitations and drawbacks of the ways in which leaders tend to think about data and the questions we ask, practical suggestions and exercises are recommended in the section that follows, to begin to consciously think differently.

- ■ *Be open to new ideas.* New ideas and new thinking often does not come naturally to everyone and can feel quite uncomfortable at first. Accepting a feeling of discomfort, and not resisting it without conscious examination by believing in something that produces a sense of order, in and of itself, may be a way to begin to accept another kind of discomfort in recognizing that there is often no pattern to statistical results, which are often random without discernable patterns.

- *Uncover potentially unconscious inclinations, ideas, or feelings about words and the ways they contribute to understanding an individual's thinking about data.* Consider the words and phrases we use to describe working with data. The words we use are often metaphors that actually describe other phenomena and may convey additional meaning of which we are not even consciously aware.
- *Reconsider questions in light of possible cognitive bias.*

Academics are trained to favor thinking that focuses on rational, linear activity over knowing through one's emotions. Yet, emotion also contributes to the way we make meaning out of our experiences. As discussed above, the randomness of data and our tendency to exaggerate the consistency and coherence of data, can lead us to make meaning that is inaccurate. Drawing on the work of Kahneman (2011), Taylor and Marienau (2016) describe a two-faceted approach to becoming more aware of one's thinking through combining two approaches: verbal-theoretical conceptual and embodied metaphorical. They then bring together these two approaches with practical activities to help uncover and move past cognitive biases. Two such activities are presented below, adapted from those offered by Taylor and Marienau (2016).

Activity

Read each word in the list in Figure 5.2. After reading each word, call up a visual image of each in your mind's eye. Draw the image that comes to mind on a piece of paper, or search the Internet for a suitable image. Consider potential alternate meanings for the images you create or find for each word or phrase. You will notice that many of these words and the related images they call up are actually metaphors that

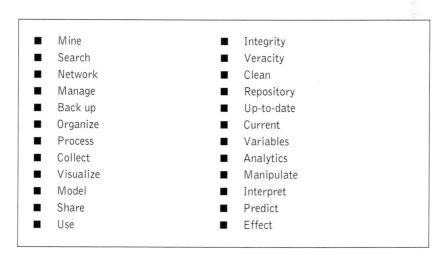

- Mine
- Search
- Network
- Manage
- Back up
- Organize
- Process
- Collect
- Visualize
- Model
- Share
- Use

- Integrity
- Veracity
- Clean
- Repository
- Up-to-date
- Current
- Variables
- Analytics
- Manipulate
- Interpret
- Predict
- Effect

FIGURE 5.2 Words Used to Describe Data Usage.

invite a particular way of thinking about data. For example, the word "mine" as in "data mining" suggests mining precious metals or stones that have high value. Through using this word or phrase about data, we may be unconsciously (or perhaps consciously) expecting that the data will provide some highly valuable information that will assist in decision-making, help explain a phenomenon, or present a solution to a problem. If one considers the likelihood of the randomness of data, one might seek a different word or phrase to describe data. The "precious gem" may not exist!

Another such word to consider in the context of talking about data is "interpret." To interpret means to translate words into another language. Using this word in the context of data may reveal that the speaker believes data is difficult to understand and requires the work of an expert in both data and plain language to convey the meaning of the data.

Upon completing the activity, note any shifts in thinking about the meaning of the words used to describe data.

This activity is best conducted in a larger group and in the context of reviewing a report about your institution's data. After the researcher or data analyst has presented the report and shared the results and conclusions, invite the entire group to reconsider the questions that were posed that prompted the study, in light of any possible cognitive bias. At this point, consider sharing about the three kinds of cognitive bias described above, or invite the group to read Tversky and Kahneman (1974), which discusses many forms of cognitive bias. After viewing the study and its results, note how the thinking of the group may have shifted and note any new questions that arise.

SUMMARY

The process of changing thinking in higher education, in the context of data culture creation is one that must be intentionally considered. This chapter suggests a four-part process in which leaders both individually and collectively engage. It begins with an awareness of the influencing factors that contribute to the data culture at an institution including higher education news sources, think-tanks, policy makers, accrediting bodies, service providers, peers, and internal stakeholders including other leaders, faculty, and boards. Next is a conscious reframing of thinking, with consideration of mindfulness techniques and uncovering cognitive bias. Testing one's new thinking in the context of the larger group of decision makers at one's institution is the third step, in alignment with the purpose and mission of an institution. Finally, the institutions' leaders consider new questions about data in the context of their goals, compliance requirements, and strategic plan. The process is iterative, such that questioning one's thinking becomes an ongoing and developmental process of continuous change, and intentional improvement.

DISCUSSION QUESTIONS

1. What did you learn about your own thoughts and feelings related to the words you use in the context of data and its use?
2. After considering the influences of others, and the ways in which cognitive bias may cloud thinking about data, how do you envision changes at your institution and the questions you ask?
3. This chapter offers several factors that influence thinking about data in an institution's culture. Which additional factors might you add to these?
4. What tools do you find work best to make you aware of your own thinking?
5. Who in your institution challenges your thinking most or the group thinking of your institution?
6. Which efforts to change thinking about data and the questions leaders ask have been successful at your institution? Which have not? Why or why not?
7. The history of higher education includes a strong focus on challenging assertions and popular notions through careful examination of evidence and an empirical approach to analysis. Why might higher education leaders choose not to take this approach to examining their own thinking and thinking about data in particular?
8. As you look toward the future of higher education and consider the trends that may continue and evolve, how might thinking about higher education data change?

REFERENCES

Dewey, J. (1910/1997). *How we think*. Boston, MA: Dover.

Ekowo, M. & Palmer, I. (2016, October 24). The promise and peril of predictive analytics in higher education. *New America*. Retrieved from www.newamerica.org/education-policy/policy-papers/promise-and-peril-predictive-analytics-higher-education/.

Fong, J. & Kovar, K. (2016, April 18) Fostering a data-informed culture in higher education. University Professional Continuing Education 101st Annual Conference. *Helix Education*. Retrieved from www.helixeducation.com/wp-content/uploads/2016/04/Fostering-a-Data-Driven-Culture-in-Higher-Ed_Helix-Education-and-UPCEA.pdf.

Hall, J. & Reim, M. C. (2017, March 28). *Time to reform higher education financing and accreditation*. Retrieved from www.heritage.org/node/132981/print-display.

Helix Education. (2017). *Enterprise Outsourced Program Management*. Retrieved from www.helixeducation.com/outsourced-program-management/.

Kahneman, D. (2011). *Thinking, fast and slow*. New York: Farar, Straus and Giroux.

Langer, E. J. (1989). *Mindfulness*. Cambridge, MA: Perseus Books.

Lumina Foundation. (n.d.). About. Retrieved from www.luminafoundation.org/about.

Massy, W. (2011). Metrics for efficiency and effectiveness in higher education: Completing the completion agenda. Retrieved from http://agb.org/sites/agb.org/files/u3/MetricsforEfficiency.pdf.

Taylor, K. & Marienau, C. (2016). *Facilitating learning with the adult brain in mind: A conceptual and practical guide*. San Francisco, CA: Jossey-Bass.

Tinto, V. (2004). Student retention and graduation: Facing the truth, living with the consequences. Occasional Paper 1. *Pell Institute for the Study of Opportunity in Higher Education*. Retrieved from http://files.eric.ed.gov/fulltext/ED519709.pdf.

Tversky, A. & Kahneman, D. (1974, September 27). *Science, 185*(4157): 1124–1131.

WASC Senior College and University Commission. (2013). *2013 Handbook of Accreditation, Revised*. Retrieved from https://wascsenior.box.com/shared/static/oxgx719tnw5bn8b4kp28.pdf.

Chapter 6

Fostering Data-Driven Leadership

Stephanie Douglas

INTRODUCTION

The paradigm shift to a data culture in higher education institutions to systematically gather and use data brings a need to develop new competencies, skills, and abilities among human resources. In fact, many institutions feel that they already have a developed data culture. Often missing from a more developed data culture is leadership. For an institution to develop a data culture or further a data culture, leadership must turn data into information and institutional knowledge through analysis and interpretation.

This shift in culture and development takes a sustained effort over a long period of time and at multiple levels within the institution. It is leadership that must take the lead to advocate for, and maintain focus on, a data culture as the mode of thinking and practice. Data-informed leadership is the drive to be objective and evidence based in decision-making. These decisions involve products (majors, programs, services), processes (registration, advising, policies, procedures), and people (faculty, staff, alumni, students, stakeholders). Data informs leaders to better outcomes, drives change, and creates new value.

Leadership is key to fostering a data culture and shaping how and why data are used and what people are aiming for with data-informed decision-making. Through use of data, statistical and quantitative analysis, explanatory and predictive models, and fact-based management, leadership can drive decisions and actions. Moving beyond data analysis, data-informed decision-making is a form of communication in which the analysis is transformed into a recommended action to guide activity. The output of the work must transform multiple, disparate, and disconnected streams of organizational data into information (for more details, see Chapter 8), upon which organizational leaders can build and implement strategies to substantially improve performance.

FOSTERING DATA-DRIVEN LEADERSHIP

If organizations are to successfully navigate the implementation of a data analytics initiative, especially one that touches the academic core, organizational leaders will need to develop a more data-informed culture and cultivate leaders with analytical skills. Engagement of academic leaders in the process is critical because they have a detailed understanding of the academic processes and decision points that would benefit from data analytics.

Simply gathering and analyzing data is not the sole catalyst for continuous improvement and institutional success—institutions have developed individuals at the analyst level, such that many institutions are quite expert in turning data into information. Leadership must use data carefully to inform decision-making as part of an ongoing process of continuous improvement. Use of data for decision-making should not be seen as a fad or something that is the latest and greatest technique.

Leaders must drive the use of data in decision-making while assessing what types of data are useful and what purposes the data will be used to inform. Specifically, within higher education institutions, data-informed leadership aims to contribute to improving the student outcomes and advancing the institution. Data must be well defined, validated, and clearly understood by the leader in order to best develop buy-in for others to utilize data in decision-making. It is vital to ensure the data are valid and useful, as bad data can lead to bad decisions. Data-informed leadership occurs when leaders systemically collect and analyze various data sets to guide decisions intended to improve the success of the institution overall.

The challenge for leaders is to reshape the central practices and cultures of their institutions to allow proactive use of data for informed decision-making. Leaders need to legitimately challenge organizational cultures that preserve loose coupling by demonstrating the value of the new data culture practices as a means to persuade staff and faculty that the change to a data culture is beneficial. Where once gut feeling and proven experience were the most important factors in decision-making, the use of data and advanced analytics identifies complex processes and interdependencies to assist in prediction and the analysis of the needs of the institution in greater detail.

The value of data-informed leadership lies in enabling evidence-based decision-making and avoiding biased judgments. Often the heart of the issue for leaders in utilizing data-informed practices is how to get people to change their behavior and use analytics in their day-to-day jobs and rely on the facts. The key leadership skills necessary for the behavior change and development of a data culture are discussed in the following section.

DATA-DRIVEN LEADERSHIP SKILLS

Table 6.1 shows a set of data-informed leadership conceptual skills. Each will be discussed in this section.

Collaboration

The core element of any successful change process is collaboration. Collaboration, combined with the purpose for change, the institution's commitment to the change and the outcome focus will lead to success. A leader will have conversations with multiple offices and departments giving the opportunity to faculty and staff to share, discuss, and ideate on the change. This is critical to gaining insights into the success factors and struggles when driving an organizational change to data culture. Being able to have people share and develop ideas to further the implementation will get their skin in the game and make them feel a part of the culture and thus supportive of the behavior change.

Authenticity

Aligned with collaboration, authenticity involves the connection of the change to the institution's culture and values in addition to a shared understanding of the purpose and meaning behind the change. Leaders gain buy-in through the collaborative efforts to build a shared understanding of the purpose of behavior changes to adopt a data culture. For the change to be authentic, its purpose must be connected to the institution's mission, vision, and overall culture. For example, an institution which is largely open access admissions advancing a data-informed retention initiative which studies the impact of ACT scores and high school GPA on first to second year retention is connected to the institution's

Table 6.1 Data-Informed Leadership Conceptual Skills

Concept	Definition
Authenticity	Shared understanding and agreement among members of the organization of purpose of innovation and outcomes designed to achieve; consistency between the project and the organizational culture and values.
Collaboration	Collaborative innovation development and adoption across the organization with decentralized and transparent decision-making responsibilities regarding implementation.
Recognition	Leaders who actively support innovation and reward adoption of the data culture as well as finding organizational resources available to support implementation.

open access admissions culture. This organizational change, driven by data, determines what additional programs and support should be in place for specific students; thus, it is authentic to the institution's mission of open access.

Employee Resources

To ensure the institution is intentionally and authentically moving in the desired direction of a data-informed culture, the solution lies in recognizing and rewarding innovative behavior supporting data-informed culture, as well as employing the resources necessary to support the change. Often employees are looking for meaning and not things. As a leader, help faculty and staff feel appreciated and understand how they like to be recognized.

Peer to peer recognition also creates a virtuous circle of meaning. Encouraging and stimulating such powerful recognition can be relatively simple, yet extremely rewarding. Providing the necessary resources for the innovation to occur is also necessary to ensure a successful change. Leaders must clear barriers and provide the necessary tools to support the change. Further details on resource development are included later in this chapter.

Leaders should obtain timely, useful information, try to understand the root causes behind the numbers (as discussed in Chapter 5), and design interventions targeted to the specific areas most likely to inhibit success. The idea is to focus both resources and efforts most efficiently where they will make the biggest difference (Slavin, Lake, Davis, & Madden, 2011), for example, using data extensively to inform strategic decision-making, but not letting data completely overrule your human instincts and experience. Organizations are best able to succeed in a rapidly changing environment by being agile, responsive, and intelligent.

Leaders can use data effectively to develop and foster a culture in which all members of the institution understand, apply, and manage data as a dynamic entity to support the institution's goals and to improve outcomes for students and staff. Development of an institution's data-informed culture is determined by the needs and resources of the institution, as well as the leader's own style. The leaders who achieve and foster this culture often achieve success using several key strategic steps as summarized in Table 6.2.

PRACTICES FOR FOSTERING DATA-DRIVEN LEADERSHIP

Table 6.2 shows a set of practices for fostering data-informed leadership. Each will be discussed in this section.

Table 6.2 Practices for Fostering Data-Informed Leadership

Leadership Practice	Description
Setting a shared vision and goals	The leader collaboratively sets a shared vision with a motivating rationale, such as equity of learning outcomes, which are connected to a measurable goal of attainment.
Questioning skills supporting data-driven decision-making	The leader employs an inquiry approach to guide the collaborative analysis of data for continuous improvement.
Leading by modeling	Leaders set an expectation for data use and provide collaborative support coupled with individualized coaching on the use of data to inform decision-making.
Developing a culture and open communication	The leader utilizes effective communication that results in a culture of trust and continuous improvement.
Providing professional development	The leader ensures staff are provided with quality, job-embedded professional development and coaching to improve data literacy.
Collaborating as teams	The leader designs collaborative teams, or professional learning communities, focused on the analysis of data to guide decision-making.

Setting a Shared Vision and Goals

A clear, shared vision of why and how data will be used to improve an organization is essential to success. This vision must relate to the overall vision of the institution set by the chancellor or president. The vision of why and how data will be used must be specific to the data culture but must also maintain consistency with the overall institutional vision and culture. Framing the shared vision of data-informed decision-making, such as equity and learning outcomes for all students, delineates a motivating rationale for the implementation of data-informed decisions, leading to a synergy that follows through all levels of leadership.

Setting measurable goals or outcomes for the use of data is a necessary component in setting a vision of effective data use. This relates back to the key leadership skill of developing a shared meaning for the data culture among the stakeholders. Shared meaning typically develops into understanding and then striving for the measurable goals or outcomes. The examination of data without a conversation of continuous improvement or analysis of needs and potential actions to address the needs would be futile.

A clear vision must present the rationale for a data culture and its benefits in order to set the stage for the work ahead. A leader should focus on clarifying misconceptions about creating a data-centric culture versus simply using an isolated set of tools or reports to provide information. This presents an opportunity for rich discussions to establish the shared vision and mission, and often provides a sense of relief to staff as they gain focus.

Questioning Skills Supporting Data-Driven Decision-Making

The practice of inquiry or questioning is necessary in leading the use of data and ultimately developing the data culture. Six categories of actions for advancing inquiry are needed to use data effectively:

1. Questioning
2. Connecting to mission
3. Analyzing
4. Connecting to organization
5. Technology competencies
6. Collaborating time with teams

Shifting to an inquiry approach in data use by posing a question or problem statement to be explored through the use of data can often ease those who are hesitant to use data in a data-informed approach. Use of questioning frames the approach into a meaningful and understandable method for exploring the initiative and then the application of data analytics (discussed in more detail in Chapter 10). Approaching data through a lens of continuous improvement and inquiry assists in narrowing the data and discussion to target the collaborative analyses on specific actionable outcomes.

Focusing on inquiry leads to higher levels of data, analysis, and decision-making. Conversely, using simple data for simple decision-making can lead to basic use but does not cultivate a data culture. Basic use of data does not solve complex problems centered on improvement, but tends to address specific questions, such as how many desks to order for a particular classroom space. The act of using data moving along a spectrum from basic use to inquiry results in outcomes that follow a spectrum from simple to substantial (Ikemoto & Marsh, 2007).

Leadership and Support

Vision and clear expectations for data use and evidence-based outcomes are important in leadership for data-based decision-making. Modeling of data-based decision-making by leaders, as well as the establishment of expectations that set performance goals, are linked to data-based inquiry which fosters the data culture. Leaders operate as coaches, functionally fostering the development of data-informed leadership in staff and other leaders. Leaders provide support and coaching in all aspects of a data culture in order to develop buy-in and support the use of data-informed decision-making. An important aspect of the coaching is framing questions that cause staff to reflect on their own practices and outcomes to begin a paradigm shift to data-informed decision-making.

Creating a successful data culture also requires leaders to provide the infrastructure to support the culture. A leader must establish a strategic relationship between administration and those overseeing critical data infrastructure, such as data warehousing. This opens the door for valuable insight on the data management systems and can maximize instructional and administrative efficiency. A data management system that provides a usable warehouse of both information and assessment data allowing for various customizable reports provides leaders with the necessary tools to lead with data.

Culture and Communication

Developing organizations that effectively use data rests on the establishment of an ethos of continuous improvement (Datnow, Park, & Kennedy-Lewis, 2013; Farley-Ripple & Buttram, 2014; Datnow & Park, 2009). Using data in non-threatening ways promotes the paradigm of data-informed decision-making for continuous improvement. Modeling effective use of data and operating as coaches in building the capacity of others contributes to the development of a data culture at the institution. By enabling others to use data-informed decisions, structured collaborative teams foster the development of trust and a culture shift. Leaders must communicate and establish motivation and meaning for the data-informed decision-making culture to become systemic and self-sustaining (Martin & Farrell, 2014; Datnow et al., 2013).

Changing an institutional culture to a data culture is not as simple as announcing a new way of doing business and expecting compliance. A key step in the culture change is to reinforce trust among staff and seek collaboration regarding the specific steps in the process, desired outcomes, and methods for implementing the change. Instigating a culture shift will likely cause a sense of fear or hesitancy about its impact on individuals' roles, responsibilities, statuses, or workloads. Examination of performance data in the absence of trust can be threatening to leaders and staff. Collaboration is necessary for the development of collegial trust in the work of data analytics.

Developing an understanding and buy-in requires continually emphasizing the importance of the change in culture and its ongoing nature. Opportunities to address obstacles and concerns, as well as celebrate successes, must be built into meetings, interactions with staff, and communications with the entire institution. The conversation and work on the transition to data-informed decision-making and a data culture needs to be part of the daily functions of leaders in all areas. Keeping the conversation going and providing momentum is required to establish that the change is not a passing fad from administration.

Professional Development and Support

Care and consideration must be given to the growth and support of staff in preparing for a new way of doing business through data-informed decision-making. Professional development is an ongoing process focusing on gathering and increasing knowledge as much as specific skills such as analytical abilities, data mining, or interpreting data findings. This development is paramount to the success of culture change. Feedback and interactions during the early development of the process offer insight into the current mindset regarding adoption of a data culture and allows for quick intervention or clarification by leaders regarding any misinformation, fears, or potential attitudinal barriers. Professional development offerings and specific training focusing on building analytical skills and how to use data appropriately must align with the institution's plan.

Staff will also need time to create their own understanding and fit in a data culture. A single training session will not provide the sufficient support or alleviate all concerns held by staff. Consistent access to development resources for building a strong foundation of comfort with the new culture is essential. The focus and training with data will also help to work through issues regarding past practices, such as decisions on gut instincts, as well as help work through organizational and behavioral changes. This also assists in promoting the sense that staff are part of the solution as they begin to create their own mindset and data culture identity.

Professional development on the best practices for using data suggests successful organizations work hard to support and empower staff to use data to inform decisions. Staff must be trained on both the data management systems and using data reports effectively. A data culture built on asking questions of data and collaboration on best practices creates improvements. The more staff are given an opportunity to analyze data as a collaborative team, the more they will realize the benefits of using data on a regular basis to inform decisions and make improvements.

Collaborative Teams

Leaders foster collaborative opportunities that offer shared learning, dialogue, and reflection from all members of the organization (Danzig, Borman, Jones, & Wright, 2006). Development of a data culture will be most useful when it is characterized by widespread involvement among faculty and staff. Collaboration is touted by many researchers as an effective general educational practice (Schmoker, 2004) and is particularly useful in promoting a data culture.

An effective leader can be seen as a community builder who has the opportunity to stretch leadership across different organizational roles to involve various players. Data use in leadership is an important element in supporting and spreading data use among faculty and staff. Engaging staff and faculty in thoughtful, collaborative inquiry in practice is an empowering act enabling them to be partners in data-informed decision-making.

To be effective, faculty and staff must see themselves not as passive, dependent implementers of someone else's script, but as active members of a data team. There are barriers that inhibit faculty and staff's development of a data culture. Leadership, as noted throughout this chapter, is key in assisting faculty and staff to overcome these barriers.

Resistance to adoption of a data culture can be because of the organizational change involved and effective data use has been shown to be too burdensome for an individual to take on without collaborative effort (Stringfield, Reynolds, & Schaffer, 2001). Solutions to these problems rely on leadership to form collaborative data use, promoting the partnership of institutional research departments with faculty and staff to effectively use data. Effective collaboration can be difficult to achieve given the educator autonomy historical context of higher education and implicit power relationships; however, effective leadership brings together the enthusiasm for data use among faculty and staff to the necessary partners on campus. This allows faculty and staff to be supported in using data, while also having the necessary resources to utilize data effectively, thus, creating an active data culture.

Collaboration for inquiry is a positive by-product of data culture initiatives but collaborations can be unfocused and not ubiquitous. Even in supportive environments, collaborative teams can be difficult to foster. Leaders need information and research on practices that can help them cultivate collaborative data teams.

Within teams, there are traits crucial to building collaboration that can also undermine the collaboration. The size of teams has increased over the past few decades as often teams are formed to ensure the involvement of a wide stakeholder group, while harnessing multiple skills. Research has found that as the size of the team increases, the level of natural cooperation among members of the team decreases (Gratton & Erickson, 2007).

Leaders should assess the team's size to ensure it is not too large, yet still includes a wide array of skills and viewpoints. As technology increases and the work environment becomes more virtual, many teams may have members who are working at a distance from one another. The value of different insights and knowledge may mean members working from multiple locations.

Research has shown that as teams become more virtual, collaboration declines (Gratton & Erickson, 2007). Regular check-ins from leadership and purposeful meetings to measure progress of the team are vital to continuing collaboration while teams may be in different locations. The diverse knowledge and views of team members can spark insight and innovation, leading to positive collaboration; however, research has shown the higher proportion of people who do not know anyone else on the team and the greater the diversity, the less likely team members are to share knowledge and collaborate.

As a leader, it is important to establish a sense of belonging to the team and also understanding of the team members. This feeling of fit among team members will help to build the collaboration and reach the ultimate goal for the team. Finally, building collaborative teams involves drawing on a variety of deeply specialized skills and knowledge to devise data-informed solutions.

The greater the proportion of highly educated specialists on a team, the more likely the team is to disintegrate into unproductive conflicts. While it is inevitable in higher education not to have highly educated specialists on the team, it is the leader's responsibility to define the roles of the individual team members, while giving the team latitude on how to achieve the task.

RESISTANCE AND MISPERCEPTIONS

The adoption and expansion of data analytics at colleges and universities can be viewed through the lens of theories on innovation diffusion. Diffusion of innovation was developed by E. M. Rogers in 1962 and explains how over time an idea or product gains momentum and then diffuses through a specific population or social system.

The end result is that people who are part of the system adopt a new idea, behavior, or product. The key is for the members of the system to perceive the idea, behavior, or product as new or innovative in order for the diffusion to be possible. Colleges and universities face complex challenges to implementing and sustaining innovations because of their approach to organizing work, resulting in failure more than success.

Utilizing innovation diffusion, leaders must organize their work to show the benefit of adopting this new culture, so faculty and staff buy in and adopt the innovation. Utilizing a directive approach or a top-down decision-making approach often hinders such diffusion. The collaborative nature described earlier in this chapter is an effective avenue to creating the buy-in and spreading the innovation diffusion.

There are many cultural and personal reasons why people struggle to rely on data to improve work. Data analytics and data-informed decision-making holds the risk of revealing new insights that can be contrary to someone's experience about how the world works. Numbers can elicit resistance; reactions may have little to do with the message and everything to do with the medium. Data can be incomplete or insufficient to draw firm conclusions, it can be easy to keep searching and analyzing in hope of achieving more clarity.

The fear of displacement can produce anxiety and cause resistance in some people. In their minds, they were hired for their experience, expertise, and gut instinct. These people may not appreciate the important synthesis of data and business understanding that is required to make analytics useful. Inexperienced users of data will often question their own ability to understand what the data means.

They wonder if their interpretation is right and how exactly to read data visualizations. Can they trust the data? Can the sources of data be trusted? Can the motives of the person who provided the data be trusted? Data-informed decision-making links data to actions and sometimes data insights are generated by a data science team, while the people at the front lines are some distance away. Relying on data can take time to find the right data, test, and evaluate the results. In the fast-moving world, to be competitive, data analysis can be seen as laborious, time consuming, and expensive. People can become fixated on the details and lose the ability to pull themselves up to a level to appreciate the implications of the details.

Understanding Reasons for Resistance and Misperceptions

As a leader, it is important to debunk the view of data as a source of negative information. When a positive data culture is established, benefits such as program prioritization and development of strategic initiatives, supported by utilizing data, are experienced by the organization and its clients. Many individuals are not comfortable with using data. They avoid using data to make decisions and view it as time consuming and neither a benefit to themselves nor to their students because of their own lack of knowledge and skill.

Data-informed decision-making as part of a data culture is fundamentally different from traditional approaches in that it is goal oriented rather than process oriented. Often institutions evaluate and adjust practices based on their direct impact rather than emphasizing certain processes and delivery. This approach directly challenges the notion of what was traditionally believed to be effective. Reliance on evidence-based practices can be perceived as reducing autonomy and depending on data that does not reflect real-world experiences.

Although many staff and faculty believe data could improve their teaching, a number feel they do not have the training or tools to use data effectively. It is also thought that the data is not sufficient to improve institutions, due to a variety of shortcomings of data tools such as easy access to useable, detailed data. This obstacle can actually reinforce the institutional and general resistance to using data, as the shortcomings of poorly implemented and ineffective data tools may cement the notion that pursing data-informed decision-making is not a worthwhile endeavor.

The lack of access to data is a significant obstacle to data use and can inhibit adoption of a data culture. Quality of the data is also a concern for those being asked to implement data-informed decision-making, such as whether test scores accurately reflect students' knowledge or whether satisfaction data derived from surveys with low response rates accurately measure outcomes. Access, as well as the doubts regarding data, are important factors affecting meaningful adoption of a data culture.

Development of robust, effective data systems depends on an institution's ability to broadly adopt the data systems. Yet, institutions are limited in their ability and willingness to adopt data systems because institutions have little incentive to disrupt existing operations and, in some instances, cultural and political pressures prevent schools from expanding their use of data. This problem is compounded by the fact that while many such systems can offer greater benefits with greater adoption, the nature of higher education with widely varying standards, budgets, technical ability, and differing policies about data collection and use limits productive efforts to coordinate its adoption.

Addressing and Overcoming Challenges

Colleges and universities develop organizational cultures that define acceptable ways for the organization to address opportunities and challenges through innovative activities and limit attempts to do things differently (Clark, 1972; Schein, 2004). Norms and expectations for using data need to be established and agreed upon by relevant staff and leaders for a data culture to be maintained (Datnow & Park, 2009). Leaders are responsible for modeling positive behavior with the use of data and building trust.

Staff will not see the benefits associated with using data, if they feel threatened or embarrassed by the results; data cannot be seen as measures that are used to label and categorize staff. Through collaborative analysis of data, staff are able to share best practices and strategies for improving the organization and meeting its goals. Knowledge creation occurs in the process of social interaction about information (Light, Wexler, & Heinze, 2004).

Providing opportunities to show that data are not being used to "get" staff or faculty but to improve the institution's success can help minimize resistance. The less resistance occurs, the more the culture helps people understand data are not being collected and analyzed to harm people. Leaders must help the institution understand that using data is a shared responsibility.

One of the primary responsibilities of a leader is to help people confront problems. The way to confront problems is to identify them and the way to identify them is by looking at data.

PRACTICAL SUGGESTIONS AND GUIDANCE

Aligned with leadership theories and team-building strategies, a successful data-informed leader will be equipped to lead a data culture. The following factors should be considered and utilized in leading the implementation of a data culture:

- *Invest in signature relationship practices.* Leaders at all levels of the institution can encourage collaborative behavior by making visible investments in a data culture that demonstrate their commitment and the institution's commitments. Providing resources for faculty and staff to utilize data, modeling data-informed behavior, and rewarding innovation and use of data can all showcase this investment.
- *Create an organizational culture adapt to data.* Leaders must act as mentors and coaches to help build the networks necessary to work across a campus and to overcome institutional barriers.
- *Ensure the requisite skills.* Leaders who invest in human resources that equip faculty and staff to utilize data set the stage for success. Teaching faculty and staff to build significant relationships with team members, develop the ability to communicate and resolve conflicts creatively through data, and feel comfortable utilizing data can have a major impact on the adoption of a data culture.
- *Understand role clarity and task ambiguity.* Data-informed teams that work collaboratively are possible when the team members understand their roles and are given the autonomy to achieve the task. If the leader creates the collaborative culture, equips team members with the skills and abilities to utilize data, and then defines the roles of the data team, it is possible to achieve the task at hand.

SUMMARY

Colleges and universities are complex in organizational, cultural, and political nature; these are all aspects which must be addressed in the use of data-informed leadership and data analytics systems. As individuals with substantial understanding of educational processes and operational decisions within higher education organizations, leaders are prime drivers of data culture. Leaders are from all divisions and departments on a campus including academic affairs, student affairs, business services, information technology, and many other departments. Through guided leadership focused on a data culture, the adaptation of the culture can be successful. The support and guidance of data-informed leadership can assist in overcoming barriers to implementation and limit misperceptions of a data culture. Building on the key leadership skills and practices discussed in this chapter, the Chapter 7 focuses on the relationship-building skills leaders need to help transform data culture.

DISCUSSION QUESTIONS

1. What is the relationship between data and accountability as a leader?
2. How does your leadership philosophy and style incorporate data-informed leadership?
3. What leadership characteristics are important in data-informed leadership?
4. When facing barriers to implementing a data culture through data-informed leadership, what are the priorities for a leader?
5. How would you describe the data culture at your institution? Identify one or two key strategies you could employ in your area to contribute to an enhanced data culture.
6. The chapter discussed six leadership practices (Table 6.2). Which of these practices resonated with you and why?

REFERENCES

Clark, B. (1972). The organizational saga in higher education. In C. Brown (Ed.), *Organization & governance in higher education* (5th ed., pp. 153–159). Boston, MA. Pearson Custom Publishing.

Danzig, A., Borman, K., Jones, B., & Wright, W. (2006). *Professional development for learner centered leadership: Policy, research and practice.* Mahwah, NJ: Lawrence Erlbaum.

Datnow, A., Park, V., & Kennedy-Lewis, B. (2013). Affordances and constraints in the context of teacher collaboration for the purpose of data use. *Journal of Educational Administration, 51*(3): 341–362.

Datnow, A. & Park, V. (2009). Conceptualizing policy implementation: Large-Scale reform in an era of complexity. In G. Sykes, B. Schneider, & D. Plank (Eds.), *Handbook of education policy research* (pp. 348–361). New York: Routledge Publishers.

Farley-Ripple, E. & Buttram, J. L. (2014). Developing collaborative data use through professional learning communities: Early lessons from Delaware. *Studies in Educational Evaluation, 42*: 41–53.

Gratton, L. & Erickson, T. J. (2007). Eight ways to build collaborative teams. *Harvard Business Review, 85*(11): 100.

Ikemoto G. S. & Marsh J. A. (2007). Cutting through the "data-informed" mantra: Different perceptions of data-informed decision-making. In P. A. Moss (Ed.), *Evidence and decision-making: 106th yearbook of the national society for the study of education, Part 1* (pp. 104–131). Malden, MA: Blackwell Publishing.

Light, D., Wexler, D., & Heinze, J. (2004). How practitioners interpret and link data to instruction: Research Findings on New York city schools' implementation of the grow network. Paper presented at the Conference of the American Educational Research Association (AERA), San Diego, CA.

Martin, J. A. & Farrell, C. C. (2014). How leaders can support teachers with data-informed decision-making: A framework for understanding capacity building. *Educational Management Administration & Leadership,* 1–21.

Schein, E. H. (2004). *Organizational culture and leadership* (3rd ed.). San Francisco, CA: Jossey-Bass.

Schmoker, M. (2004). Tipping point: From feckless reform to substantive instructional improvement. *Phi Delta Kappan,* 85: 424–432.

Slavin, R. E., Lake, C., Davis, S., & Madden, N. A. (2011). Effective programs for struggling readers: A best-evidence synthesis. *Educational Research Review,* 6: 1–26.

Stringfield, S., Reynolds, D., & Schaffer, E. (2001, January). Fifth-Year results from the High Reliability Schools project. Symposium presented at the meeting of the International Congress for School Effectiveness and Improvement, Toronto, Canada.

Chapter 7

Building Relationships

Karinda Rankin Barrett and Eric Godin[1]

INTRODUCTION

In today's era of accountability, higher education institutions are increasingly called upon to justify their decisions. While issues of access, enrollment, and size are historic measures of institutional success, higher education has now shifted to a prioritization of student completion and job attainment (Bailey, 2016). Twenty years from now, a new focus may dominate the halls of America's higher education system.

Regardless of how institutions are evaluated now or in the future, the age of anecdotal decision-making is fading and leaders must now have evidence-based solutions. Whether developing a new ten-year institutional strategic plan or joining a national college initiative, data are vital to an institution's ability to demonstrate its effectiveness. Institutions that embrace a culture of evidence and use data to inform decision-making will find themselves leading the field ahead of changing tides, rather than being reactive to currents they cannot control.

Maxwell and Person (2016) wrote that, "Current comprehensive reform efforts call for colleges to build a culture of evidence that uses data to continuously assess programs and processes against student success, suggesting changes when benchmarks are not achieved" (p. 7). Comprehensive reform requires a culture of evidence as well as a focus on measurable student outcomes and a cohesive program for changing the student experience (Bailey, 2016).

Creating a culture of data-informed decision-making is a journey built on relationships and sharing. To move past the lack of systemic and significant improvement in student success (Stout, 2016), campus leaders must learn to engage with each other and build off each other's strengths. An entire campus must be engaged in meaningful work to produce significant change.

In the past, reform initiatives were based on a limited focus and often involved a small group of leaders. As Bailey (2016) shared, "small pilots can rely on a small group of activist faculty, administrators and stakeholders who are enthusiastic about reform, and they can be carried out without disrupting normal practices at institutions" (p. 16). To change culture and move to a foundation for data-informed decision-making, relationships need to be deep and engaging to move beyond discrete interventions. Further, engaging stakeholders across campus, in the community and beyond expands work to include areas outside of the academic experience.

In the past, access to data and the analytical tools needed for analysis have been maintained by a small group, who provided services and support to the campus. With the shift in access to data, opportunities exist to reframe the use of data and the roles of those who traditionally were the keepers of data. Research units are challenged to add capacity by leading and teaching others how to engage with data (Swing & Ross, 2016).

National discussions about the nature of institutional research (IR) have aided campus reform efforts by portraying IR professionals as critical partners in this work. For example, Voorhees and Hinds (2012) wrote that: "Institutional researchers should be comfortable existing at, and reaching across, boundaries to help the institution accomplish its strategic goals" (p. 76).

Professionals within an institution embracing a culture of evidence interact and develop culture through a shared vision, data-focused initiatives, professional expertise, diverse thinking, open dialogue, and overcoming challenging personalities. Institutions can cultivate and harness the power of critical thinking, as well as analytical reasoning, at the campus level. This framework, as illustrated in Figure 7.1, provides the key elements for a data-informed environment and serves as a guide for the chapter.

DEVELOPING A SHARED VISION

Developing a shared vision begins with a leader who challenges his or her team to spread and direct the vision. To illustrate, Chancellor Hadley at Tarrant Community College took personal responsibility for the success of the college's Achieving the Dream Initiative. She modeled her expectations by visiting each campus where she ensured financial and moral support.

She took a hands-on approach to share and engage the entire college leading to systematic and transformative change (Wilson & Bower, 2016). Such a shared vision should include questions for guiding the work. For example, one college continually asked what was best for students and how did the work impact student success, completion, and retention (Wilson & Bower, 2016).

A shared vision is critical to the success of selecting the right purpose and goals. In the past, reforms were too discrete and targeted components of a process as opposed to the overall student experience (Bailey, 2016). Using data to share a story will engage others and focus attention on the relevancy and

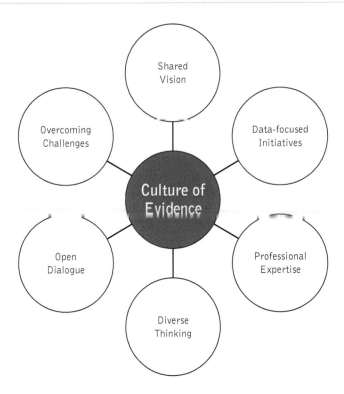

FIGURE 7.1 Relationship Focused Characteristics of an Institution Embracing a Culture of Data Evidence.

usefulness of relationships built around data. Relationships need attention, focus, and must be prioritized to develop.

Relationships formed around the relevancy of the work tend to be most productive. Progress occurs as the culture shifts when the team is successful and builds confidence by reaching milestones, overcoming conflict, and benefiting from the success resulting from the use of the data. Setting expectations for a shared vision defines a structure for culture where data is central to success.

DATA-FOCUSED INITIATIVES

The environmental context, including national initiatives, legislation, and institutional strategic plans, dictate the need for building strong, effective relationships. A successful culture of evidence requires people at all levels of the organization to take responsibility for each aspect of the culture and complete the process of continually creating, collecting, analyzing, evaluating, promoting, and using data to improve desired outcomes. "Changes are more likely to occur within organizations when the leadership encourages shared decision-making and provides members with opportunities to make sense of information and the implications for practices" (Jonson, Thompson, Guetterman, & Mitchell, 2017, p. 36).

The priorities established through a national agenda all the way down to a college or university's strategic plan define the need for relationships to plan, implement, and evaluate initiatives as well as everyday operations. To adapt to changes when benchmarks are not achieved, relationships benefit from honesty and a willingness to assume the various perspectives needed to adjust the culture and direction of work. Open attitudes and behaviors receptive to feedback enhance the adaptability of the institution.

Accountability programs such as Achieving the Dream and striving for awards such as a Bell Weather or an Aspen Award, which recognize outstanding programs within community colleges, create motivation for intentionally redesigning culture to a data-informed decision-making environment. For example, Tarrant County College realized the impact of the Achieving the Dream initiative as one that changed the college and everyone involved to a single focus with one purpose, one goal of increasing student success through data-informed decision-making (Wilson & Bower, 2016). External coaches engaged with the campus to guide the work and provide an alternate, unbiased perspective. Through each of the programs, feedback originates from external sources and potential relationships with national and regional colleagues may leverage a central focus on data.

Accrediting agencies have implemented stronger accountability related to student outcomes, dictating that faculty collaborate and work together to review student success, ultimately using feedback to revise outcomes, enhance teaching and learning and review, as well as improve, assessments. With the accreditation paradigm shifts focusing on accountability and improvement, collaboration throughout higher education institutions requires the development of relationships and clarification of roles. As the perceived potential internal utility of assessment evidence increases, faculty and staff are more likely to engage in relationships and build teams to review the work.

When the institution creates an environment integrating and internalizing processes dictated by external entities, the assessment loop is more likely to close and lead to a deeper level of student success (Jonson et al., 2017). Although issues with closing the loop remain, questions arise as to who is on the team and what roles should be fulfilled by additional colleagues. According to Jonson et al. (2017), "reports suggested that faculty involvement in assessment must increase as institutions evolve from a culture of compliance to a culture of evidence-based decision-making if the use of assessment findings to improve teaching and learning is to become more common" (p. 35).

PROFESSIONAL EXPERTISE

Understanding the environmental context leads to a foundation for determining who should be part of the team and defining roles for building a culture of data evidence where professional expertise is valued. In addition to those within the institutions, those outside the college or university may also serve as effective partners for moving the campus forward in terms of integrating data and expanding usage. Those involved may include district administrators, board members, campus leaders, faculty and staff (Wilson & Bower, 2016). K-12 colleagues also provide valuable information and data on incoming students (Stout, 2016).

Seasoned vendors make a compelling case for using data to unify and focus efforts on success. Vendors often understand the need to use data to demonstrate return on investment. Those leading national initiatives such as data coaches and researchers are invaluable partners for providing technical assistance along with an unbiased perspective on how relationships need to progress to remove barriers and focus on the primary vision of the college or university (Bailey, 2016).

Institutional research (IR) offices are often involved in projects during the analysis and review of data. Including staff from IR as team members throughout projects provides an opportunity to strengthen processes and data collection, as well as the analysis of the results (Goomas & Isbell, 2015). A team approach from planning to implementation and through evaluation enriches the work with various perspectives. Goomas and Isbell shared an example of a service-learning project lacking a central repository for tracking data as well as an inconsistent way of tabulating across the institution. This is an example of where involving IR and other departments throughout a project would reduce time and effort in analyzing and reviewing results. Additionally, a combined team approach has the potential to result in robust data, deepening understanding of the results.

DIVERSE THINKING

A strong network requires members from all roles and departments in the institution with diverse perspectives and ways of thinking. Faculty from different departments, administrators, staff from institutional effectiveness offices, instructional designers, librarians and other support staff need to participate to enhance the culture and completely integrate the use of data throughout the institution. Additionally, those who lead from where they are, regardless of job titles and position authority, may be the most effective at mobilizing others. The challenge is to identify those who can easily integrate changes into their own work and express a desire to lead others in a culture of change.

Faculty tend to work in isolation based on the nature of their positions and responsibilities (Jonson et al., 2017). In the past, reviewing student outcomes was limited to the faculty member's own classes and typically did not involve colleagues. The focus on accountability requires a vulnerability on the part of faculty to be open to feedback to advance student success. Further, faculty may feel pressure for student grades to be within an expected range when comparing courses to one another.

Accountability is the opportunity to receive feedback from others and implement improvement—a noble goal, albeit one that is contrary to previous work and the lives of faculty members. Building collegial relationships among faculty and institutional effectiveness staff leads to cultural changes and shifts to a new way of helping students succeed.

Faculty lack of expertise with assessment is often a barrier to engagement (Jonson et al., 2017). As experts in their fields, faculty may be reluctant to venture into a subject such as assessment with which they have little context. The key to success in working with faculty is to demonstrate the benefit of building relationships to make data-informed decisions to enhance student success.

When colleges bring faculty, staff, and administrators together, perceptions change and data are more likely to be used as a mechanism for improving student learning (Jonson et al., 2017). For example, at one institution, workshops brought faculty together for cross-discipline discussions on prerequisites. Relationships formed in the workshop led to a better understanding of student expectations and faculty worked together to address student gaps in learning. Because of the workshop, a physics professor and a dental hygiene professor worked on a project to develop students' understanding of how X-rays work.

In another situation, faculty reviewed prerequisites for a math class and determined the prerequisite course was unnecessary because the course did not contribute to student success in the following course. The prerequisite was eliminated, saving students money while reducing the time to graduation. In both examples, the convening of faculty, both cross-discipline and within discipline, as well as the time to build relationships and discuss issues led to enhanced student success.

Fostering relationships and setting institutional expectations for engagement on critical topics leads to improvement. In one department, units meet weekly to discuss and review how data is collected and used. This work has led to the improvement of processes, communication, and support for other entities outside of the department. Further, the quality of the data, relevancy, alignment with beliefs, policy, and practice as well as actionability will determine how likely information is to be used for improvement of student success (Jonson et al., 2017). Alignment indicates the need for strong cross-department and functional job positions to ensure consistency as well as standardization of work. "The

key to a college's effectiveness is how well it aligns and manages all of its programs and services to support student success," (Goomas & Isbell, 2015, p. 493).

Another example of the importance of data-based relationships happened
with a president's executive team. When members of the team wished to
propose new projects or initiatives, the president always required data as the
basis for the decision. Similarly, throughout the implementation and evaluation
of the project or initiative the president required data to continue conversations
and understand progress.

OPEN DIALOGUE

Communication and open dialogue flourish when channels are clearly given the
time and space to develop. Each member of the institution brings a unique set
of skills and abilities that contribute to the success of students and the college.
Working together, the team can cultivate these skills and relationships. Kirby
and Floyd (2016) noted that developing relationships with functional offices is
essential to effectively responding to and solving institutional challenges.

The first step in effective communication and open dialogue should be understanding the organizational structure of the institution. This is essential because the
direct line of reports for college departments indicate the importance of these
offices. For example, an office of institutional research reporting directly to the
president with a seat on the president's cabinet may be viewed with more importance and significance than the same office reporting through another department,
such as Business Affairs, Student Affairs, or Information Technology.

Although a recent survey by the Association for Institutional Research (AIR)
found that reporting lines of IR offices are not predictive of the office's relationship with the institution (Swing, Jones, & Ross, 2016), the way college staff
interact with and have access to offices of IR will vary based on reporting lines.
Therefore, while the organizational structure may not impact the relationships
of senior leaders, implications may exist for other staff members. By understanding the structure of the institution, staff will find themselves in a better
position to determine whom to talk to about specific projects and initiatives.

Once the appropriate staff members are identified to assist with a project or
initiative, the next step is to learn about their skills and opportunities for further
professional development, which will be mutually beneficial. For example, academic affairs staff can provide additional context to data requests, while data
analysts and institutional researchers can assist academic staff with understanding the nuances of higher education data and statistical analysis. Voorhees and
Hinds (2012), wrote that: "Institutional researchers can accelerate the development of actionable data, but this requires a commitment to open dialogue across
the campus and, often, a willingness to visit other units to form a deep understanding of the issues they face" (p. 75).

Terenzini's (1999) foundational work on organizational intelligence in the field of institutional research can be easily applied to other professions. He proposed that institutional researchers move through three sequential tiers of organizational intelligence as they progress in their careers. The first tier, technical/analytical intelligence, includes factual and methodological knowledge—the basic skills of the profession. The second tier, issues intelligence, brings an understanding of important processes and policies. The third tier, contextual intelligence, is "the form of intelligence that earns institutional research and researchers legitimacy, trust, and respect" (p. 25) because it demonstrates a professional's technical and issues intelligence, within the context of both an individual institution and the history of higher education. Academic affairs staff have no doubt gone through similar steps in their own careers. The point is that institutional researchers can assist academic affairs leaders with increasing their intelligence around data, just as academic affairs professionals can assist the IR community in increasing their organizational intelligence.

Finally, standing meetings create an expectation for ongoing communication and continuous opportunities for discussions. Meetings without a defined purpose and agenda should be avoided, as they can become viewed as a wasteful use of resources. Instead, a strategy for how teams work together, identify actionable items, and hold themselves accountable should be developed. Disagreements will occur and when dealt with in a professional manner, can improve relationships by providing an opportunity for colleagues to highlight their expertise. Voorhees and Hinds (2012) suggest that IR offices should be impartial and provide object clarity and that institutional researchers are strategically positioned to serve as servant leaders, helping to provide data and information, but also steering open discussions. This concept could be extended to any office that provides data.

OVERCOMING CHALLENGES

Working with a diverse group of professionals is one of the most challenging and rewarding aspects of a career in higher education. The differences between new and seasoned administrators, educational backgrounds, professional expertise, and philosophies on education bring a myriad of lenses through which professionals interpret the educational process and work. When conflict occurs, productive teams step back from the situation and determine the cause. Understanding the reason for disagreeing with a colleague is the most effective way to arrive at a mutually agreeable solution. In general, challenges arise from: 1) a lack of understanding; 2) belief that one's own methods are absolute; 3) unwillingness to try something new; and 4) politics.

Challenging personalities sometimes stem from a lack of understanding regarding the purpose, methods, and benefits of a specific initiative. Colleagues may not be able to see the vision because of a limited perspective and realize the true potential of the proposed work. When this occurs, relationships benefit when more information is shared about the work and the connection with the larger project. For example, a data analyst compiling information on enrollment intensity changes between the first and second semester of a student's college career may not realize the importance of full-time enrollment during a freshman's first year and its impact on that student's persistence and eventual graduation. Providing this larger context educates the data analyst and allows colleagues to see how their work can impact student success.

There will always be individuals who assert that their way of thinking is absolute and that their methods for solving a program or addressing a campus issue are ideal. In these cases, an effective strategy is to allow the individual to explain their position and then others may work to provide evidence-based support for an alternative viewpoint. While this individual may be leading a committee or project and has the authority to overrule, documenting alternate ideas illustrates professionalism and these ideas may be useful later.

Professionals who have been working in the field for several years in the same position or office may become used to doing things the same way each year. Also known as SALY (same-as-last-year), this method for completing tasks is a barrier to innovation and progressive thinking. Professionals are more inclined to think this way when their work is not respected or utilized. For example, an annual report for a grant program may be a mundane task year-after-year. However, sharing the information widely, discussing and using the data for programmatic change, increases the relevancy and importance of the work. When leaders praise good work and explain how the data will benefit the college and the community, morale increases and strengthens relationships.

Finally, politics plays an important and often overlooked role in campus decision-making. Over time, colleagues develop relationships and mutually beneficial points of view. Whether overt or covert, these personal friendships and arrangements may influence projects or committee decisions. More than one higher education professional has explained that their role as a committee chair is to steer the group to a specific decision, while at the same time making the team think they came to the decision naturally. The impact of how politics influence outcomes can be positive, negative, or neither, depending on a team member's perspective. Higher education professionals need to recognize how campus politics may impact their work and determine if it is advantageous to take a side.

What happens if a colleague is unwilling to work with others in a positive manner? In these cases, a few options exist, such as leverage from senior administrators and incentives. The quickest way to ensure campus-wide buy-in on an initiative or project is the support of the president and senior administrators. Commitment from senior leaders solidifies the college's investment and signals the importance of the work. In other situations, incentives may be the best option. Initially, external incentives may be needed to engage faculty and work toward an internal willingness to engage. Alternatively, a colleague may offer to help another department with one project for assistance with another department's projects.

PRACTICAL SUGGESTIONS AND GUIDANCE

Figure 7.2 provides practical suggestion and guidance for building a culture of evidence. Each is described in this section.

- *Engage the board.* Those who strategically lead and govern the college or university should be involved in the early process of developing relationships to support a culture of data evidence. As champions of the college or university, board members need to understand data as well as the benchmarks and milestones the institution is striving to reach. Reviewing data and related initiatives are often standing agenda items for board meetings (Wilson & Bower, 2016). Additionally, community college board members need to reflect the aspirations of the community they serve. Their challenge is to ensure the primary vision and mission of the college focuses on student success rather than local priorities (Stout, 2016).
- *Involve the entire college.* For colleges with multiple campuses and centers, involving the entire college presents a greater challenge but is worthy of the effort to include multiple perspectives. Bringing together those who typically do not have the opportunity to engage and interact reduces the typically siloed nature of higher education.
- *Prevent initiative fatigue.* Recent reform has happened through a variety of initiatives and often overwhelms faculty as well as staff (Wilson & Bower,

- Engage the board
- Involve the entire college
- Prevent initiative fatigue
- Constantly review processes and procedures
- Infuse data into the relationship
- Connect with state and federal colleagues
- Lead the initiative
- Prioritize professional development

FIGURE 7.2 Practical Suggestions and Guidance for Building a Culture of Evidence.

2016). A reduced capacity for new initiatives leads to resistance for engaging in the important work of developing a culture of evidence. Those leading the cultural paradigm shift gain support by outlining the specific benefits of using data-informed decision-making and showing the effectiveness of the work.

- *Constantly review processes and procedures.* Colleges should review processes and procedures on a regular basis to determine what is working and consider possible adjustments to streamline the future work and continue to build relationships. "Substantial improvement requires a continuous process of reform and assessment of evidence of improvement that must become embedded in the college culture" (Bailey, 2016, p. 17).

- *Infuse data into the relationship.* Leaders set the example by using data every day (Rorison & Voight, 2016). Building relationships around data includes bringing and reviewing data regularly. Use data to guide the conversation and inform the development of questions, the identification of issues, and the direction for addressing problems by determining data-informed solutions.

- *Connect with state and federal colleagues.* State and federal colleagues collect, use, and review data from a policy perspective (Rorison & Voight, 2016). Insights will broaden the work of the college or university through benchmarks with national and state data. Furthermore, state and federal colleagues connect with other entities as well as offer a framework for strategically aligning with state and national priorities.

- *Lead the initiative.* Undertaking a shift to a culture of data evidence must be the primary focus of the president of the college or university. Although many aspects of the shift must be delegated and infused into the operational work of the college or university, the president must take the lead for setting the vision and the culture of the institution to set a mission explicitly valuing data-informed decision-making and a culture of data evidence (Stout, 2016).

- *Prioritize professional development.* As the culture is developing, faculty, staff, and administrators need new tools and frameworks for understanding and functioning in a shifting environment. Colleges and universities are often understaffed in critical areas such as IR and benefit from boosting related knowledge and skills across the campus. "In addition, stress from retirements and transitions in the pipeline of presidential and academic leadership are creating a crisis of continuity on many campuses making a sustained focus on student success nearly impossible" (Stout, 2016, p. 106). Professional development allows the time and resources to enrich talent and prepare people to compete for open positions, while infusing the culture to move the college or university to a more comprehensive impact on student success through data-informed decision-making.

SUMMARY

In summary, building a culture of data evidence begins with the president of the college or university and is heavily dependent on the leadership team's ability to engage campus administrators, faculty, and staff as well as those at the local, state, and national levels. Relationships need expectations, focus, and time to thrive, while constantly working to enhance and drive the primary mission of the college and university, which is the improvement of student success and outcomes.

DISCUSSION QUESTIONS

1. What drivers in the environmental context can be used to leverage relationships for building a culture of evidence?
2. Which of the strategies for building effective relationships will improve your institution's culture and success?
3. How may your team strengthen your institution's primary mission?
4. Considering the importance of communication and open dialogue, what expectations should your institution establish?
5. What are the next steps for your institution to establish or enhance a shared vision?
6. How can you better address issues related to challenging personalities?
7. What practical suggestions or guidance are most effective for your college for building relationships given your current position?

NOTE

1. The opinions expressed in this work are that of the authors and in no way represent the views of either author's current employer or other entities.

REFERENCES

Bailey, T. (2016). The need for comprehensive reform: From access to completion. *New Directions for Community Colleges, 2016*(176): 11–21.

Goomas, D. T. & Isbell, A. (2015). The challenges of institutional research in building a culture of evidence: A case study. *Community College Journal of Research and Practice, 39*(5): 489–494.

Jonson, J. L., Thompson, R. J., Guetterman, T. C., & Mitchell, N. (2017). The effect of information characteristics and faculty knowledge and beliefs on the use of assessment. *Innovative Higher Education, 42*(1): 33–47.

Kirby, Y. K. & Floyd, N. D. (2016). Maximizing institutional research impact through building relationships and collaborating within the institution. *New Directions for Institutional Research, 2015*(166): 47–59.

Maxwell, N. L. & Person, A. E. (2016). Comprehensive reform for student success. *New Directions for Community Colleges, 2016*(176): 7–10. http://onlinelibrary. wiley.com/doi/10.1002/cc.20217/epdf.

Rorison, J. & Voight, M. (2016). Leading with data: How senior institution and system leaders use postsecondary data to promote student success. Retrieved from www.ihep.org/research/publications/leading-data-how-senior-institution-and-system-leaders-use-postsecondary-data.

Stout, K. A. (2016). Implementing comprehensive reform: Implications for practice. *New Directions for Community Colleges, 2016*(176): 99–107.

Swing, R. L. & Ross, L. E. (2016). A new vision for institutional research. *Change: The Magazine of Higher Learning, 48*(2): 6–13.

Swing, R. L., Jones, D., & Ross, L. E. (2016). The AIR National Survey of Institutional Research Offices. Association for Institutional Research, Tallahassee, Florida. Retrieved from www.airweb.org/nationalsurvey.

Terenzini, P. T. (1999). On the Nature of Institutional Research and the knowledge and skills it requires. *New Directions for Institutional Research, 1999*(104): 21–29.

Voorhees, R. A. & Hinds, T. (2012). Out of the box and out of the office: Institutional research for changing times. In R. D. Howard, G. W. McLaughlin, & W. E. Knight (Eds.). *The Handbook of Institutional Research* (pp. 73–85). San Francisco, CA: Jossey-Bass.

Wilson, D. & Bower, B. (2016). Steps toward transformation: One college's achieving the dream story. *Community College Journal of Research and Practice, 40*(11): 965–967.

Chapter 8

Managing Complexity and Chaos

Kristina Powers and Paula S. Krist

INTRODUCTION

Turning data into information is complex. Working with people can be unpredictable. Combining these two elements—creating information and working with people—creates a complex and often chaotic environment. If not managed properly, this can lead to wasted resources in the form of duplication of work, decisions being made based on wrong information, as well as dissatisfied and frustrated employees and leadership.

Leaders of higher education institutions are under an enormous amount of pressure to make the "right" decision and be accountable to all stakeholders: students, parents/family, elected officials, accreditors, state agencies, etc. When making these decisions, timeliness is a critical factor by which leaders are judged by (Kiel, 1994), which contributes to the chaos because time is limited. In the end, leaders are trying to focus on the institutional mission and do the best they can with the resources they have, while finding the pinpoint of common ground of all stakeholders that will be acceptable. This is done for every decision that leaders make!

Let's turn to the role of data in leaders' decisions. Most people come to work wanting to do the right things. Leaders want to make the best decisions possible and will utilize any and all information they can to make the best decision; based on the information available at the time a decision needs to be made. Institutions have a lot of data and leaders have many ways to obtain data.

The Need to Turn Data into Information

Data alone is not sufficient—it must be turned into information. Data that is information is one key element for decision-making. For example, a course roster of all students in all sections of math courses and their course grades cannot be absorbed for decision-making until it is analyzed. Analysis could include descriptive statistics or statistical analyses. The chief academic officer likely does not have the time to perform this work on his/her own. Thus, leaders need to rely on data analysts to perform this work.

Often leaders are presented with a problem to solve and they have limited time to gather information to make a decision. However, leaders who have never been responsible for turning data into information or direct management of people who do this work often do not have an understanding of the time, effort, and energy required to produce a deliverable under the best of circumstances (i.e., clear requirements, sufficient time to do the work, and skilled person to do the work). In fact, many leaders may think that the work can and should be done faster, often asking "what is taking so long?". As a leader, the question was simple—"What were the last three years of retention rates by college for students receiving federal financial aid?". So why is this request taking more than 20 minutes to complete?

This chapter addresses these three main issues for leaders: problems that are causing chaos, strategies for managing the chaos as it relates to data, and how to effectively communicate with people performing or hindering the work. The goal of this chapter is to provide leaders with greater understanding into the challenges associated with getting the information they desperately need in a timely manner, and strategies for altering the approach and/or management of the data functions to eliminate or reduce those challenges so as to yield more timely results for decision-making. Additionally, understanding the challenges from the perspective of the data function and the employees who work in those groups will garner leaders greater trust and respect from data analysts, which translates into better work and more timely deliverables.

What is the Chaos Problem?

No one means to create confusion, but most institutions suffer from some degree of it. There are several ways that chaos can develop in an institution of higher education and all of them can affect the decisions made by the institution's leaders. There are ways to reduce or eliminate some of the chaos that will be addressed later in this chapter. First, let's look at some of the reasons that chaos and complexity arise.

What causes the search for data in the first place? At a professional meeting, an institutional leader may use data to illustrate how his or her institution is excelling in some way. A news or journal article may present some statistics that make another institutional leader want to know "Is this true for us?" or "I wonder how we compare?" Sometimes, the leader may be following a "big idea"—considering changes before the idea has been benchmarked or any research has been conducted.

Naiveté Causes Chaos

Some of the situations that create chaos stem from naiveté on the part of an institutional leader, who might be new at the institution or new in a leadership position (for more information on knowing the context, see Chapter 3). Higher education leaders may not know which people or offices to ask when they have a question. In some instances, chaos can arise because whoever is asked tries to answer it—because the president, provost, or other leader has asked them for it.

The person or office that is asked may try to figure out how to obtain the data themselves. In other situations, data, even data from the best source, may be provided without context, leading to incorrect conclusions. Offices that are supplying data may also have new data managers or analysts, who are not yet able to examine the data within the institutional context. They may not be able to convert data into information.

Because they work with data and data systems, one might assume that information technology professionals understand data better than other areas of the institution. Some of them may even have the word "analyst" in their job titles. Their functional roles may not require familiarity with higher education or educational analyses; thus, they have limited context for information needs.

Firmly Planted in the Past

Conversely, chaos and confusion can arise because various offices of individuals at an institution may not have evolved as new data management techniques and systems have come on line. They may be remembering how things were organized or managed at another time; this can hinder their ability to determine the best source of information. Also, people who have worked at the institution a very long time may tend to respond anecdotally, without data or real evidence, at all.

Too Much Data

Another cause of confusion, discussed in detail in Chapter 9, is too many potential sources of data. This can occur because of differences in how data is managed at different institutions. For example, maybe the Registrar's Office handled something at a previous institution and Institutional Research provides that information at the current institution. An institutional leader, particularly one who is new in a position, may make assumptions that lead to data that do not address the real questions being asked. This problem can be compounded by the fact that the information is needed quickly. The president is giving a speech tomorrow or the board of trustees wants to know a particular data point (e.g., how many students have registered for next semester already) before next week's meeting. Asking multiple sources for the same information or "shopping around" for information may seem like the fastest way to get information, but can lead to conflicting, confusing, or inaccurate results.

Often an institution has multiple data management systems, for example: one system for student records data, one for finance and budgeting, and another for human resources data. Then there are systems that extract data and data warehouses in which data are stored. Additional systems track student learning outcomes, faculty qualifications, and tenure and promotion records. Although there are exceptions, many of the systems do not integrate with others. Some institutions have systems that have been modified or customized to work for their specific needs. These systems tend not to be able to update or add on without additional customization.

The data in one system may not agree with the data in another system, for example, business intelligence (BI) systems pulling data from a transactional data warehouse may be pulling real time, up-to-the-minute data. BI systems pulling data from a warehouse built on official census data will have numbers that are always the same for a given time frame—and they will not be a match for transactional data. These "data disconnects" can cause confusion and may engender distrust of one or more sources of data. Data from any source must be presented within the institutional context. Otherwise, an institution can suffer from too much data and too little information.

Table 8.1 shows the discrepancies between transactional and official data. While both numbers can be accurate, there are standards, norms, and protocols for external reporting that ensure consistency. Chaos and confusion can be reduced, if individuals are specific in what they ask for and analysts are specific in labeling the materials that they provide. As shown in Table 8.1, the official reporting date for enrollment for this sample institution, is October 20. Thus,

Table 8.1 Data Comparison

Week	Sample Enrollment	
	Transactional	Official
September 1	10,032	
September 8	10,123	
September 15	10,089	
September 22	10,062	
September 29	10,022	
October 6	10,021	
October 13	10,018	
October 20	10,016	10,016
October 27	10,015	

reported externally, the enrollment will be 10,016. However, if an administrator asks for the current enrollment just one week later, he/she could be provided a different number, 10,015 as of October 27, simply because transactional or official enrollment was not specified.

Lack of Knowledge

Most institutions have some degree of chaos or confusion created by people's ignorance or behavior. Those who work in higher education, more than in other fields, tend to reinvent the wheel. Instead of first determining if the answer to a question is already known, they tend to develop a way to find out the answer themselves.

As an example, the president wants to know how the institution compares to peer institutions on a metric just released by a national newspaper. He asks the vice-president of public relations, who deploys four staff members to develop a list of peers and consolidate the metrics from the article into a table. The Public Relations office develops a peer list that does not match the list the institution uses for other comparisons. Nor did they realize that the table cited in the article could be downloaded for ease of use.

In this case, a lot of time was wasted that could have been avoided with some internal research before jumping to respond. In another instance, a faculty member wants to know something about students at the institution, so she creates and distributes a survey before determining if the information she is seeking is already known. This kind of "rogue" behavior can result in the distribution of results that are insufficient or inaccurate. Those being surveyed may develop survey fatigue from too many surveys, or become frustrated by questions that ask things that are already known by the institution, such as demographics or the number of academic majors.

Reducing the Chaos

How can chaos and confusion be minimized? How can institutional leaders get the information they really need? There are institutional strategies that can be implemented to assist with these important issues. These may be summed up within three sets of strategies: managing data users, managing data chaos, and managing data and users.

MANAGING DATA USERS

Both complexity and chaos must be considered when working to accommodate the people who use data. Examine the possible causes of the chaos: data confusion, conflicts, and insufficiencies. Determine where leaders typically go to find

101

information; create an inventory of these offices and their key personnel. Collect examples of how data is communicated.

Power Users

A starting point is to elevate the importance of data accuracy, consistency, and security at the institution. One way to address this is to form a group comprising institutional data custodians (e.g., registrar, information technology, institutional research), key data managers (e.g., admissions, registrar, information technology, finance, financial aid, institutional research), and institution decision makers and other data "power users."

This is a group that needs to be connected, to understand and sometimes to set the policies and procedures surrounding data management and maintenance. Forming this data group will shift the institutional culture in some important ways. First, it will reduce and possibly eliminate siloes that exist between the groups. For example, when analysts from the Admissions Office, the Registrar's Office, and the Information Technology personnel who work with the student information system collaborate, it will enhance the accuracy of student records.

Second, the information needs of the institutional leaders will be clearer to those who input, maintain, and harvest that data. If all of these people are on the same page, data stored in systems will be more accurate and will require less cleaning when it is retrieved to be used for informing institutional leaders. Third, new policies or procedures and changes in existing ones can be shared among the group. Fourth, this group, or a subgroup, can set data standards for the institution. Finally, this is a huge brain trust, a group of people who can solve problems collectively in a way that no one area could do independently.

Establishing Rules of Engagement

Institutions need to establish clear guidelines for data searching and share these strategies with campus leaders. As implied above, the first question on this list could be: "Which office is most likely to have the answer to my question?". The guidelines can include descriptions of the kinds of information that are available and the contact information for the office that is the right one to ask.

All groups to which a data question may be posed should be well versed on what data are best obtained from other areas of the institution. This is not to suggest that the data requestor be shuttled from office to office (even if it is via email). The first referral should be the final referral. Development of a set of Frequently Asked Questions (FAQs) with answers to the most commonly asked institutional questions can help offices answer common questions appropriately. Ideally, the FAQs are a collaborative effort from an array of institutional stakeholders that are involved in creating or using the information.

Creating charts, graphs, or tables that present the answers to the most commonly asked questions at an institution could reduce the complexity of the data. In addition, posting reports that summarize and contextualize data can facilitate all data seekers' understanding of what the data mean.

Clarity for Reducing Chaos

For an office answering data requests, developing the art of clarification can be a great time-saving strategy. For example, even as simple a question as "How many students are enrolled at this institution?" is really not as straightforward as it seems. Is the leader who asked the question interested in the number of students enrolled at this moment, the official census enrollment, the number reported to the federal government's Integrated Postsecondary Education Data System (IPEDS) report? Or is the leader looking for the number of undergraduate students, the total number of students, the number of degree-seeking students, the number of full-time and part-time students, etc.? Office directors should consider two methods for improving clarity.

The first step is to develop a specific request queue or a dedicated email address that is for data requests; requests are filtered by the person in charge of requests to the person in the office who is best equipped to respond. This permits prioritization of requests and consideration of other reporting responsibilities (i.e., to the federal or state governments, accreditors, other external requestors). The second step is to develop a standardized set of questions that can be posed to hone data requests to a more precise level.

For data to be used effectively at an institution, a shift to a culture of evidence-based decision-making must occur. This culture places data in context and also considers its limitations. The next section discusses effective use of data so to manage the chaos created by data.

MANAGING DATA CHAOS

Managing data is critical. It is perhaps the most vital aspect of managing the chaos and confusion that can surround it. The first step is to understand the institution's data culture. Is data currently used to inform decision-making? Who are the primary data consumers? Which areas are the data custodian(s)?

Clear and Murky Requests

Even with the most clearly defined requirements, requests can get chaotic quickly, leading you in unintended directions. For example, when there are missing data that are critical to the analysis, one may need to find a proxy variable, or replace the missing data with estimations for the analysis. Any detour in fulfilling the data request adds time and complexity—often neither was planned.

Add in murky requirements and now you likely are going in even more directions with the data—simultaneously! For example, the chief academic affairs officer emails to ask you for the latest retention rates by the end of the day. That's it—no more information. Does s/he mean rates using federal definitions, counting only first-time full-time students? How about rates by academic program? Did s/he also want graduation rates? For what period of time?

To respond to the retention request, one could produce anywhere from a lengthy response to something as simple as "the latest published retention rate is 58%." The former could have you spinning and scrambling to pull together a lot of information in a short period of time—with the hope that something in the sea of reports will satisfy the requestor. The latter could annoy the chief academic affairs officer, if that does not meet his/her needs.

Building Relationships

One of the ways that successful leaders manage this type of chaos is to build relationships with regular requestors. Knowing the requestor's prior asks, current challenges, and projects provides insight into what s/he may be "really" requesting. For example, in building a relationship with the chief academic affairs officer, you know that s/he attends every faculty senate meeting. You check the faculty senate meeting schedule and see that on the agenda tomorrow is "Improving Retention and Graduation Rates by College." Based on this information, you can "manage the chaos" and focus your energy on what the chief academic affairs officer will need for that meeting—retention and graduation rates at the university, college, and program levels.

Without having built a relationship, you could have swirled unnecessarily, creating your own chaos that did not have to happen. Thus, when building relationships, it is important to understand the meetings, events, issues, challenges, successes, etc., that are part of that person's role. What is their background? What do they value? Do they prefer detailed reports or executive summaries, tables, or graphs?

Standards and Shared Definitions

Experienced administrators and data users in higher education have multiple examples where they received two different numbers to the same question. This is extremely frustrating for all parties involved: the administrator who does not know which number is right; and the two people who provided the numbers who do not understand why the requestor asked two people to do the same work. Now extra time must be spent to "defend" their methodology.

Ideally, a person should be able to ask multiple people the same question (hopefully not at the same time to avoid wasting data resources) and get a consistent answer. Consistency occurs when all data users are using the same set of standards and shared definitions. Thus, when the chief student affairs officer asks how many students have paid their housing deposit, whether s/he asks the director of housing or the director of institutional research, both should arrive at the same number because they used the same definitions and standards. Other common standard variables to discuss are start date, GPA overall versus GPA in the major versus GPA of last thirty credits, current major versus first major, current address versus first address, etc.

Shared Data Access

We increase our chances of managing chaos, if we reduce the number of different data systems that people use. Rather, by providing data users with shared access to the same data systems, any two people, skilled at retrieving data and understanding the data they are extracting, should arrive at the same number. Chaos begins to develop when someone is asked for data for which they have some information, but could piece together multiple data files they have access to in order to answer the question. Or perhaps worse yet, someone has their own "shadow database" with information that no one else has and is not updated regularly with the institution's main student information system. Thus, the "shadow database" has inaccurate or out-of-date data that they use to create reports for administrators to use when making decisions.

Work Together—Avoid Shopping Around

Asking data analysts in multiple departments to work on the same—or near same—request is referred to "shopping around for the data answer you want." As noted earlier, this is very frustrating for the analysts who work on the request. However, this chaos, too, can be managed or avoided by connecting with the offices related to the topic. For example, Institutional Research and Admissions may be asked to provide a current count of applications. Institutional Research may pull the count of current applications, while admissions may provide the number of started (but not yet completed applications). Both are right, but why add chaos to the mix by having different numbers?

Instead, Institutional Research should, as a standard practice, reach out to area or subject matter experts to involve them in developing the report and data to be pulled and to review the output to ensure all are in agreement with how the information is labeled and displayed. As a result, both numbers could go into the response to offer a comprehensive report, rather than a limited view of applications. Ultimately, both parties, Institutional Research and

Admissions, are likely going to have to work together to resolve the number differences.

Thus, it makes more sense and reduces chaos, to start with the end—work together and avoid the shopping around. This also benefits the requestor in that they receive one final report that is thorough and all parties agree to the information in the report, rather than the administrator having to serve as an investigator to find out whose numbers are right and whose are wrong.

PRACTICAL SUGGESTIONS AND GUIDANCE: MANAGING DATA AND USERS

Managing data or users on their own is challenging; managing both simultaneously is exhausting. Pulitzer Prize Winner and Wellesley College President Margaret Clapp spoke of major problems in higher education in her American Council on Education keynote speech—including managing information and people in effective ways that advanced student and institutional success (Clapp, 1962). Even though her article was written more than sixty years ago, the problems still ring true today—albeit more modernized to include management of data and technology in addition to people. In this last section, we aggregate some practical suggestions and guidance for managing both.

- *Build relationships with key people in various areas.* While there is an entire chapter in this book about building relationships that goes into further detail (Chapter 7), it bears repeating here. Relationship building leads to trust, which allows for greater synergy and better work products than working alone.
- *Identify the "purple people" in your university.* Eckerson defines these employees as people who "see connections and possibilities that others miss. They speak multiple languages and gracefully move between groups and norms. They continuously translate, synthesize, and unify" (2012, p. 1).
- *Try to understand other people's perspectives.* Many people in higher education often feel that others do not understand their role, position, or complexity of the work they do. As a leader, tap into your empathy skills to understand the data analyst's perspective and challenges. There is usually considerable interest from the data analyst to understand the leader's perspective and challenges as that information provides context so that they can deliver a better product.
- *Create a group of "Power Data Providers."* As discussed earlier in this chapter, administrators are often frustrated by not knowing the "right" person to go to for the data. And data people are frustrated that the administrator went somewhere else for the information. In creating a group of the managers of the key areas that provide the majority of the data, leaders effectively create a one-stop data shop (without any reorganization). Additionally, by sending the questions

or data request to the "Power Data Providers" group, administrators are being open and transparent, giving the request to the *group* to decide how the group will collectively and comprehensively provide a cohesive response.

■ *Create a "Who's Who Data Directory."* Part of many administrators' frustrations is that they do not know who to go to for answers to their questions. Many administrators tend to be a repeat customer of those individuals who get the job done, perform quality work, and are good to work with. This doesn't mean they have the right answers. By creating a directory of who the data providers are and the types of work one can and should seek out their assistance with, administrators will improve the likelihood of working with the subject matter experts who best know the answers to their questions. A sample is shown in Table 8.2.

■ *Commit to not shopping around.* Shopping around creates distrust and frustration for duplicate work. As a senior leader, if you really are serious about improving the data culture and reducing your frustration, create a "Power Data Providers" group and challenge your co-workers to join you in not shopping around.

■ *Create a culture of data integrity.* All data custodians should agree to work together to ensure that data are as accurate as possible.

■ *Publicize what is already known and available.* Part of managing the chaos is sharing information to avoid duplication of work and data myths (e.g., a large majority of students are leaving the Business College because of the GPA requirement). Therefore, widely publicize existing information so as to educate others—both internally and externally—ending meaningless debates and moving on to solve actual problems.

■ *Establish processes and share them.* What is the protocol for releasing information? Which office has the honor of sharing the latest retention and graduation rates first? Establishing processes for sharing information helps to manage the chaos so that the information is accurate rather than simply reported by whoever was able to respond the fastest.

Table 8.2 Data Directory

Department	Department Head	Email	Data Scope	Data Website/ Intranet
Institutional Research	Karyn Smith	KSmith@ University.edu	Official External data, general data statistics, federal and state reporting	University/ IR.edu
Student Affairs	Joe Jones	JJones@ University.edu	Extracurricular participation characteristics, Housing data	University/ SA.edu

■ *Practice patience and persistence.* Sometimes the wheels of change grind more slowly in higher education. Continue to be a champion of positive change and don't be frustrated if change takes time.

SUMMARY

The culture of higher education institutions regarding data is shifting. Institutions that are able to be nimble and responsive to culture shifts will be more successful than those that are not. The use of data as information that drives decision-making is integral to this success. Thus, managing the complexity and chaos—both of data and people—is a worthwhile investment of time.

This chapter discussed the challenges and issues associated with managing the chaos so to provide background and context for helping to solve those problems. Solutions were offered throughout, as well as an aggregated list of practical suggestions and guidance. More frequent successes will be achieved when people are able to focus on their work rather than battling the chaos.

DISCUSSION QUESTIONS

1. What is the most frustrating situation you have ever faced when trying to get the answer to a data-related question?
2. Who are the data custodians at your institution? What data does each of them oversee? Do they work in the same data management system? How do data custodians interact?
3. Where are the "data disconnects" at your institution?
4. Who are the "Power Data Providers" at your institution? Who has the ability to bring this group together? What challenges should this group address?
5. As a requestor of data, what two changes can you make about your requests to make them less murky for the data analyst?
6. Recall an experience that you have had regarding data chaos. What went wrong? What went right? What two practical suggestions and guidance could you have employed to make the situation less chaotic for all involved?

REFERENCES

Clapp, M. (1962). Major problems in higher education. In R. F. Howes (Ed.), *Vision and purpose in higher education* (pp. 5–13). Washington, DC: American Council on Education.

Eckerson, W. (2012). *Secrets of analytical leaders.* Westfield, NJ: Technics Publications, LLC.

Kiel, L. D. (1994). *Managing chaos and complexity in government.* San Francisco, CA: Jossey-Bass.

Part III

Perceptions, Usability, and Communication

Chapter 9

Determining Appropriate Data Sources

Eric S. Atchison

INTRODUCTION

Consider the first weeks of a semester within a postsecondary institution. Students are shuffling their schedules to be flexible with work and other extracurricular activities. Soon after the institution's enrollment census date, the vice-president for academics asks department chairs for enrollment reports by program. Several departments reach out to the institutional research (IR) office, which reports official institution data. Other departments utilize methods to calculate the number of majors enrolled, like running a pre-established report within the administrative data system or counting majors on course rosters. At the next meeting of academic officers, the data are discussed and the IR director notes several discrepancies. Because of the differences in methodologies, the reporting of majors is inconsistent and the vice-president becomes frustrated.

Problems such as these may arise if multiple data sources are used and similar requests yield different results. When multiple reports are generated for the same metric with differing results, a loss of credibility can occur (Kirby & Floyd, 2016). While inconsistencies in reporting enrollment may not result in major issues if recognized, other misreporting can have larger impacts, especially when information is distributed to a wider audience. As the practice of data-informed decision-making expands in higher education, it is imperative the right data are being used to answer questions.

A key driver of developing a strong data culture requires having a clear understanding of the various data sources within the institution. Data are utilized to make decisions across most functions within an institution and these data sources are used each day to perform administrative functions and non-administrative functions. This chapter will provide an overview of understanding the common sources of data within institutions of higher education so decision makers will know the type of information that is typically and expediently available and have a framework for determining the appropriateness of a data source. First, a brief background of data reporting within postsecondary institutions prepares us to further discuss the importance of appropriate data. Next, a synthesis of typical data sources within institutions is presented. Then, a discussion of a process for determining appropriate data sources is described through identifying the data, evaluating relevance, determining availability, and documenting limitations. A discussion of data-related roles imperative to data management and governance is presented to understand how working with others is important to select and use data. To close this chapter, practical suggestions and guidance for working with various data sources as well as several questions for further discussion are provided. Scenarios will be presented to elaborate on concepts presented throughout the chapter.

FORCES AFFECTING DATA COLLECTION WITHIN HIGHER EDUCATION

A discussion of data sources would be incomplete without discussing the various forces that affect the data collection efforts within postsecondary institutions. Much of postsecondary data and information is collected as a result of questions asked outside the scope of a single office or institution. These forces can be understood as external and internal to the institution (Figure 9.1). Frequently, a combination of external and internal forces can also result in changes to the data collection activities within higher education institutions. In the following section, a discussion of both of these provides helpful information for contextualizing how these forces shape data collected within institutions.

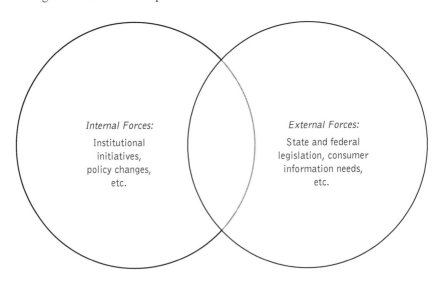

Internal Forces:
Institutional initiatives, policy changes, etc.

External Forces:
State and federal legislation, consumer information needs, etc.

FIGURE 9.1 Internal and External Forces Directing Data Collection Efforts.

External Forces

Examples of external forces are federal legislation, which may result in data collection changes within the Integrated Postsecondary Education Data System (IPEDS) (National Center for Education Statistics, 2016a), and other advocacy, policy, or consumer-oriented data collection efforts (Atchison & Hosch, 2016).

The Department of Education, where the IPEDS is located, has collected statistics on education since 1870 (National Center for Education Statistics, 1993). Postsecondary enrollment and degrees conferred have been collected since soon after the end of World War II with modifications to address relevant issues over time. An early example of expanding data collections to respond to external forces is the addition of race and ethnicity to enrollment and earned degree surveys in 1976. The IPEDS now collects information on student admissions and enrollment, awards conferred, graduation rates, student financial aid, human resources, academic libraries, higher education finance, and other institutional characteristics (National Center for Education Statistics, 2016a). Changes to the IPEDS directly impact the data collection and reporting efforts within postsecondary institutions receiving federal financial aid. Proposed changes are discussed within IPEDS Technical Review Panel meetings and are driven by "legislation, emerging areas of concern in postsecondary education, and an ongoing goal of decreasing reporting burden while retaining the federal data necessary for use by policy makers and education analysts" (National Center for Education Statistics, 2016b). A report of the National Postsecondary Education Cooperative (Aliyeva, Cody, & Low, 2018) provides origins and backgrounds of the IPEDS components and provides an extensive view of how this information is collected and made available to the public.

Numerous non-governmental external entities collect and distribute information about postsecondary institutions and students. While the purposes for these efforts may differ, the type of information collected is not static. Much of the information published is intended to create an informed consumer with information about higher education (e.g., a potential student, their parent, high school counselors, or individuals dedicated to the educational success of students). For example, the first edition of US News & World Report Best College Rankings were based entirely on academic reputation. However, the 30th edition of these rankings lists seven areas of consideration, including academic reputation and graduation/retention rates tied for the most weight (22.5%). Other data assessed for these rankings include faculty resources (20%), student selectivity (12.5%), financial resources (10%), graduation rate performance (7.5%), and alumni giving (5%) (Boyington, 2014).

These changes require additional time and effort within postsecondary institutions to collect and provide this information and may cause consumer confusion, if the data elements are not directly relevant to the institution's mission

(Carpenter-Hubin & Crisan-Vandeborne, 2016). Efforts of the Common Data Set (CDS) Initiative (2017) to alleviate duplication in reporting to external entities for consumer information have provided some relief. Some CDS data elements are infused within several of the common publisher surveys (e.g., Barron's, Peterson's, *Princeton Review*, US News & World Report, etc.). However, consumer-oriented data collection efforts continuously try to distinguish themselves and the proportion of the CDS questions within these external surveys varies (Carpenter-Hubin & Crisan-Vandeborne, 2016).

Internal Forces

In the prior section of this chapter, a discussion of external forces was presented. Internal forces at the institution also impact the data collected and reported. As higher education evolves, institutional entities have begun to collect more data relevant to institutional initiatives, academic needs, or administrative functions. We will now discuss a process to determine the appropriate data source within an institution. This consists of four steps which are: 1) identification of a data source; 2) assessment of the relevance of the data; 3) determination of availability of the data; and 4) documentation of limitations of the data source (see Figure 9.2).

Identify a Data Source

The first step to determining appropriate data sources is to identify the various functions which collect and manage data within an institution. Table 9.1 provides a list of possible administrative functions within higher education

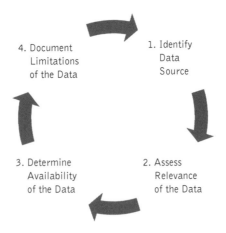

FIGURE 9.2 Steps to Determine the Appropriateness of a Data Source.

Table 9.1 Administrative Offices which may be Sources for Institutional Data

■ Academic Affairs	■ Campus Security	■ Public Relations
■ Accounting	■ Career Services	■ Registrar/Records
■ Admissions	■ Continuing Education	■ Sponsored Programs
■ Alumni/Foundation	■ Financial Aid	■ Student Affairs
■ Athletics	■ Finance	■ Veterans Services
■ Business Services	■ Library Services	■ Workforce

institutions. Some of these administrative offices are conventional sources for administrative data within higher education such as academic affairs, business services, and financial aid. In other words, for the institution to operate, information about the academic offerings and faculty characteristics, the financial records, and sources of student financial aid must be collected.

Other administrative offices in Table 9.1 may have external forces which drive specific data collection efforts. For example, a campus security office may collect information to comply with reporting requirements of campus crime statistics described in the Clery Act (US Department of Education, 2016). Data collection efforts within an alumni/foundation office may be driven by internal stakeholders, who wish to track alumni support initiatives and endowment campaign efforts. A blend of internal and external stakeholders may drive data collection efforts as well. A career services office may assist students with job placement and this information can be reported to the executive administration to ensure program completers are employed. Also, external program accreditors require information on career outcomes of graduates (US Department of Education, 2017a). Thus, many data collection efforts within an institution may have a blend of internal and external constituents.

Differentiation of administrative operations may be determined by the mission of an institution. For example, a two-year institution which provides workforce training and prepares students for academic transfer to four-year institutions may have an office focused on collecting and disseminating data on program length and program attendance (US Department of Education, 2017b). A four-year institution whose mission is to provide baccalaureate and graduate degrees and promote research activity may have an office to assist researchers in locating sources of funding and reporting information required by federal agencies, such as the National Science Foundation (NSF, 2017).

Another strategy for identifying data sources can be found through examining the institution's governance. Institutions that report data to a system, coordinating, or corporate office may already have an established protocol for reporting (L'Orange, 2008). These inventories can provide guidance of the data collected and definitions for these data elements. Data dictionaries may also reference external data definitions, which strengthen use and reliability.

While administrative data are collected to fulfill business operations (Administrative Data Liaison Service, 2016), non-administrative data also exist within higher education institutions. Non-administrative data may be collected within an institution to answer questions about program quality, institutional effectiveness, etc. These data may not be collected within a single office but across multiple offices, such as each academic department collecting separate course evaluations. Each department may have a separate form or external entity providing this service. Another example of non-administrative data is graduation surveys completed by students prior to commencement. These survey data may solely be accessible within an office of alumni affairs, career services, institutional research, etc. Non-administrative data are typically isolated within a unit and not accessible on the institution's enterprise reporting platform.

Assess the Relevance of the Data

Once a data source has been identified, a close examination of the relevance of the data source for the analysis must be done. Assessing the relevance includes examining the quality of the information, being able to access the data, and determining if the information answers the questions being posed. Knowledge of the accuracy and reliability of the data being collected is key to having confidence in using the data in decision-making.

To illustrate the issue of quality, a scenario may be helpful. As of 2011, reporting of IPEDS race and ethnicity categories has expanded to allow for self-reporting of two or more race categories (US Department of Education, 2007). At a fictitious institution, the departmental administrative assistants are responsible for updating student contact and demographic information and students are directed to them when updates are needed. One departmental administrative assistant for Social Sciences has noticed that student race/ethnicity data is missing for several students when updating their contact information. Instead of requesting the students self-select an appropriate race/ethnicity category, they select a category for them based on personal observation. This practice has occurred for several years.

Recently, a dean requested a report on student enrollment by race/ethnicity to examine racial diversity across majors within the institution. The initial report shows a variety of race/ethnic categories but a further aggregation by majors within the Social Sciences shows no students reporting race/ethnicity unknown and very few students reporting two or more races compared to other departments. Further investigation of these anomalies reveals the practice of assigning race/ethnicity to the students by the administrative assistant. At this point, the quality of the race/ethnicity data is called into question. For this example, you may decide to caution the use of the race/ethnicity data for decision-making since a systematic process for updating student data has not been established within the institution.

Another aspect of relevance is to determine if data are accessible. This can be considered a two-part process. Generally, data related to student academic activity like course registration, grades, etc. are available to these individuals for internal reporting purposes. A data source may not be available to a requestor within the institution, for example, an institutional research analyst, due to the sensitivity of the data. Other data, such as student health records or some financial aid data (e.g., family household income), may not be available to individuals at the institution employed outside of the offices, which collect this information. There may be restrictions based on job level and the organization's hierarchy that prevent some employees from having access as well. Additional criteria for access exist for individuals outside of an institution. The Family Educational Rights and Privacy Act (1974) protects student educational records and provides guidance on the release of directory information without a student's consent. For the purposes of external research requests, institutional review boards are established within postsecondary institution to "review research protocols and designs and ensure the protection of the rights of human subjects" (National Science Foundation, n.d.). Depending on the origin of request for information, there may be protocols and policies that need to be addressed prior to having access to certain information.

Determining relevance requires one to ensure that data answers the question being posed. While this might seem an unnecessary step, it is important to remember that multiple forms of the same data may exist within an institution. For example, consider a student's address. A student may have many different addresses within a single institution's data system, such as: 1) an address submitted at the time they applied to the institution; 2) a current address for the term which they are enrolled, similar to a dorm or off-campus housing; 3) a billing address for the payment of tuition and fees; and 4) a permanent address where their parents can be contacted, etc. If the director of alumni affairs requests current student addresses, any of the aforementioned data sources could be provided, but some may not be appropriate, based on the intended use of the data. This provides an opportunity to discuss the purpose of the request to determine how the data will be utilized. If the director wants to keep parents informed by sending an alumni magazine, the permanent address may be most appropriate. However, if the director wishes to send birthday cards to students, the current address for on- or off-campus housing may be most useful. This scenario is one of many that may occur within an institution and the purpose of the request typically determines the appropriate data type.

Determine the Availability of the Data

To determine an appropriate data source, understanding the availability of information is critical. This stage requires communication with the office(s) that

119

are responsible for collecting and disseminating this information as well as planning for working with those who are requesting information. Institutions often designate official information based on a specific moment in time. Many in higher education are familiar with the example at the beginning of this chapter of reporting official enrollment as of a census date. However, census dates extend beyond the enrollment of an institution and may include other data types such as staff headcounts, financial position, or student financial aid periods.

Returning to the first scenario presented in this chapter, if the communications office wants to do a press release on the official enrollment count for this term, you may want to inform them of the official enrollment census process and when the data will be available. Doing this reduces the risk of having multiple enrollment figures published in the public domain, which can cause confusion. If a separate office wishes to know current enrollment, not for public dissemination, then you can either provide the official census figure or provide the current enrollment figure with notes that distinguish this information from the official census enrollment to be reported later.

Some data types may be continuously updated during a particular time. For example, institutions may study whether a student is at risk of failing a course or not being retained. This analysis may incorporate several types of data from across an institution such as student demographics (Grebennikov & Skaines, 2009), previous academic performance, self-efficacy, and preferred learning style (Burton & Dowling, 2005). Other factors may include information that can change frequently. One example could be the number of days which a student participates in an academic support lab. Thus, recognizing that some data are static and others are dynamic can affect which data are used. The subsequent use of the data may impact the interpretation of the findings of an analysis.

Document the Limitations of the Data

The next step has been mentioned in previous sections but has not been directly discussed. Another key step when working with data in general but specifically for determining appropriate data is to document the limitations of a data source. These limitations could be associated with the relevance or availability of the data source. One example of documenting limitations for an issue related to availability could be when an institution reviews data to support the strategic plan's goals and objectives. If licensure exam data are unavailable, this data source has limitations that must be addressed. The preparer of the report should document the most recent data are included and when the updated information will be available.

Limitations of data sources due to quality of the data also should be documented. Caveats and explanations of when to use caution when interpreting data can be very helpful in ensuring the proper use of data. Returning to the first example of reclassifying race and ethnicity, this issue, if undocumented, may result in different interpretations of these data, which can impact the understanding of the student population. Consider the amount of attention placed on student success by gender and race/ethnicity (Allison, 2016; Shapiro et al., 2017; Musu-Gillette et al., 2017). The inaccuracy of this information could result in decisions about resources at your institution. Thus, clear and articulate statements about the limitations of these data allow for better understanding of how the data can and should be used.

VALUE OF SUBJECT MATTER EXPERTISE

Determining the appropriate source of data takes the cooperation and communication of individuals across administrative functions. Working with others at your institution is integral to ensuring data are identified and used appropriately. Prior to determining the appropriateness of a data source, one should understand the data structure through the process of how data are maintained and changed. This management of data within institutions can take several forms (Yanosky, 2009). Regardless of the data governance structure, individuals typically take on roles of responsibility and knowledge within the institution.

Within an individual unit, a data expert may be identified based on their knowledge and skills. For example, in a financial aid office, the staff member with the responsibility of oversight regarding federal student aid may be considered the data expert for this area. Conversely, another staff member may be responsible for institutional grants and scholarships. Depending on the scope and depth of the administrative unit, several different people may serve as data experts. Data stewards are also relevant to a discussion about data structures since they typically promote the appropriate use of data within an institution. EDUCAUSE (2015) defines data stewards as those "provide university-level knowledge and understanding for a specific data area." Communication with data experts and data stewards can promote data use and expedite the process to determine the appropriate data source.

An institutional data governance committee may comprise data experts and data stewards across an institution and have a variety of responsibilities. One responsibility could be to have formal communication and planning regarding changes to the institution's data system. The committee may also be charged to enhance the quality and oversee access to data fields. Additionally, data governance committees may be tasked to develop new data fields, since there may be relevance across offices and they may be used across the institution.

New data fields may be developed based on forces which are internal and external to the institution. The characteristics and performance of first-generation students that have been a topic of interest (Pascarella, Pierson,

Wolniak, & Terenzini, 2004), but this information may not be readily available at the institution. The Free Application for Federal Student Aid (FAFSA) has a field for highest level of education for a student's parents, but the information may not be collected at the level of detail needed for an institution for several reasons. First, if a student does not complete a FAFSA or does not complete the first-generation section, the data will not be collected. Second, the levels of education completed collected on the FAFSA may not be specific enough for the institution's needs (e.g., identifying specifically if a certificate, associate's, or baccalaureate degree earned). Third, stipulations regarding the use of first-generation data from the FAFSA may limit analysis of this information (US Department of Education, 2017c). Limitations such as these may require an institution to develop their own data fields to identify first-generation students. Working within a data governance committee to define and identify data elements can enhance understanding of student populations and help to improve program offerings and outcomes.

PRACTICAL SUGGESTIONS AND GUIDANCE

Several action steps can be taken to improve the data culture from a data source perspective (see Figure 9.3).

- *Discuss the data.* Improve relationships with others at your institution by discussing the data collected and maintained by their offices. Understanding how someone within a finance office works with data can help inform your understanding of the availability and limitations of these data.
- *Consider the big picture.* Work to have a broad understanding of the institutional data structure and how fields interact with others. Going beyond data expertise in one area is helpful to connect the work that you do to other offices.
- *Develop documentation.* Document processes related to data management and governance. These efforts can help to contextualize further developments and provide valuable background information to future efforts.

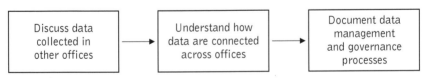

FIGURE 9.3 Suggestions and Guidance for Improving a Data Culture.

SUMMARY

A data source may impact the way information is consumed and the subsequent decisions that are made. This chapter described several steps related to identifying and vetting data sources. Also, concepts related to data governance, data roles, and working with others have been connected to the process of determining appropriate data sources. It is difficult to assess data sources without having an understanding of the governance and management of data within an institution. Practical suggestions for determining quality and availability through working with others at an institution provide a framework for determining appropriate data sources. This foundation allows for appropriate use of data for informed decision-making.

DISCUSSION QUESTIONS

1. What are several external and internal forces that have contributed to the data structure at your institution?
2. To what extent is the data system documented within your institution?
3. To what extent are administrative and non-administrative data accessible to others within the institution?
4. Is there a process established at your institution to verify data from multiple offices?
5. Reflect on institutional policies for data management and governance. What procedures are in place to establish new data elements?

REFERENCES

Administrative Data Liaison Service (2016). Administrative data introduction. Retrieved from www.adls.ac.uk/adls-resources/guidance/introduction/.

Aliyeva, A., Cody, C., & Low, K. (2018). *The history and origins of survey items for the integrated postsecondary education data system* (NPEC 2018–023). Washington, DC: National Postsecondary Education Cooperative.

Allison, T. (2016). *2016 State Report Cards*. Washington, DC: Young Invincibles.

Atchison, E. S. & Hosch, B. J. (2016). Benchmarking—Current availability, possible new national alternatives, and making a contribution to the discussion. *New Directions for Institutional Research, 2015*(166): 73–87.

Boyington, B. (2014, September 9). Infographic: 30 Editions of the U.S. News Best Colleges Rankings. *US News.* Retrieved from www.usnews.com/education/best-colleges/articles/2014/09/09/infographic-30-editions-of-the-us-news-best-colleges-rankings.

Burton, L. J. & Dowling, D. G. (2005). In search of the key factors that influence student success at university. Proceedings of the 2005 HERDSA Annual Conference, Sydney, Australia, 68–78. Retrieved from http://eprints.usq.edu.au/753/.

Carpenter-Hubin, J. & Crisan-Vandeborne, L. (2016). Guidebooks and rankings: The value of optional external reporting. *New Directions for Institutional Research, 2015*(166): 89–99.

Common Data Set Initiative (2017). Common data set initiative: Noteworthy items. retrieved from www.commondataset.org/.

EDUCAUSE (2015). Establishing Data Stewardship Models. EDUCAUSE Center for Analysis and Research. Retrieved from https://library.educause.edu/~/media/files/library/2015/12/ewg1514-pdf.pdf.

Family Educational Rights and Privacy Act of 1974, 20 U.S.C. § 1232g (1974).

Grebennikov, L. & Skaines, I. (2009). University of Western Sydney students at risk: Profile and opportunities for change. *Journal of Institutional Research, 14*(1): 58–70.

Kirby, Y. K. & Floyd, N. D. (2016). Maximizing institutional research impact through building relationships and collaborating within the institution. *New Directions for Institutional Research, 2015*(166): 47–60.

L'Orange, H. (2008). Unit record data systems: A state perspective. Retrieved from www.sheeo.org/resources/publications/unit-record-data-systems-state-perspective.

Musu-Gillette, L., de Brey, C., McFarland, J., Hussar, W., Sonnenberg, W., & Wilkinson-Flicker, S. (2017). *Status and trends in the education of racial and ethnic groups 2017* (NCES 2017–051). US Department of Education, National Center for Education Statistics. Washington, DC. Retrieved from http://nces.ed.gov/pubsearch.

National Center for Education Statistics (1993). *120 years of American education: A statistical portrait.* Retrieved from http://nces.ed.gov/pubsearch.

National Center for Education Statistics (2016a). *Media primer* (NCES 2017–047). Retrieved from http://nces.ed.gov/pubsearch.

National Center for Education Statistics (2016b). Changes to the 2016–17 IPEDS Data Collections. Retrieved from https://surveys.nces.ed.gov/ipeds/ViewContent.aspx?contentId=17.

National Science Foundation (n.d.). Human subjects. Retrieved from www.nsf.gov/bfa/dias/policy/human.jsp.

National Science Foundation (2017). Research performance progress report screenshots and instructions. Retrieved from www.research.gov/common/attachment/Desktop/NSF_RGov_RPPR_ScreenshotsandInstructions.pdf.

Pascarella, E. T., Pierson, C. T., Wolniak, G. C., & Terenzini, P. T. (2004). First-Generation college students. *The Journal of Higher Education, 75*(3): 249–284.

Shapiro, D., Dundar, A., Huie, F., Wakhungu, P., Yuan, X., Nathan, A., & Hwang, Y. A. (2017). *A National View of Student Attainment Rates by Race and Ethnicity—Fall 2010 Cohort* (Signature Report No. 12b). Herndon, VA: National Student Clearinghouse Research Center.

US Department of Education (2007, October 19). *Final guidance on maintaining, collecting, and reporting racial and ethnic data to the U.S. Department of Education*, 72 Fed. Reg. 202.

US Department of Education (2016). *The handbook for campus safety and security reporting.* Washington, DC: Office of Postsecondary Education.

US Department of Education (2017a). *Current practice of recognized accreditors student achievement standards.* Retrieved from www.ed.gov/accreditation.

US Department of Education (2017b). *NSLDS Gainful Employment User Guide.* Retrieved from https://ifap.ed.gov/nsldsmaterials/010617NSLDSGEUserGuide.html.

US Department of Education (2017c). *Guidance on the use of financial aid information for program evaluation and research* (PTAC-FAQ-9). Retrieved from http://ptac.ed.gov/toolkit.

Yanosky, R. (2009). Institutional data management in higher education. Retrieved from https://library.educause.edu/.

Chapter 10

Making Data Practical and Engaging

Angela E. Henderson and Resche D. Hines

INTRODUCTION

We are no longer in the age of data exploration; the primary driver of how we interact with data lies in our ability to perceive and navigate the data. Today, data are everywhere and seemingly relatively accessible. The floodgates of data have opened, creating new and different complexities. This increased data availability has in turn made it more difficult to convey meaningful information. As Bock (2015) observed, "the more information you're dealing with, the more difficult it is to filter down to the most important bits" (p. ix).

Organizations have historically framed decision-making from a linear lens grounded in the 20th century, based on limited ability to access data. This is largely due to the slow advancement of innovations in dissemination of data, which have lagged advances in data accessibility. Despite data becoming more accessible, there remained a lag in organizations' ability to disseminate data clearly in non-linear methodologies. As a result, data have been primarily disseminated in two-dimensional frameworks designed to answer a single question. In our world, questions and data have become more complex, multi-dimensional, and multifaceted than a singular framework can effectively portray. The traditional singular linear methodological framework creates gaps/delays in responding to subsequent questions prompted by the data, hindering the user ability to explore and leverage data for deeper decision-making.

Institutions seeking to promote a data-informed culture must strive to develop data structures and reports, which shift from static data reporting to interactive data exploration. Institutions which couple visualization with intentional user experience are able to provide engaging data with accompanying contextualization to help users understand the reasons behind past, current, and future trends (Simon, 2014). Yuk and Diamond (2014) similarly noted that institutions which employ interactive data visualizations promote individual data exploration and encourage collaboration based on a shared understanding of the data (Yuk & Diamond, 2014, p. 18). This approach advocates a comprehensive nature of data dissemination, contextualized and structured to provide meaning for the complexities and multifaceted nature of modern questions. Simply stated, the modern challenge is no longer how to find and access data, but rather how to synthesize, contextualize, and disseminate data effectively to answer multiple questions, which drive the organization. How, then, does an institution shift from a culture of flat data to one of robust data?

To achieve this shift, institutions must foster data-informed cultures grounded in frameworks that allow key stakeholders to clearly understand appropriate questions and how data articulate insights to address these questions. Nested in these frameworks, communicative vehicles must be developed that allow institutions to seamlessly visualize and make meaning of multifaceted complex data and data sources. There must be an intentionality about how institutions think, design, and structure visualized data to inform decisions and facilitate active learning for all key stakeholders. The ability to nimbly grow and learn while leveraging data are the key components to robust institutions and informed constituents. Before actions to encourage a shift toward a data culture can be implemented, an understanding of the right questions and of the existing user expectations and influences must be examined.

USER EXPECTATIONS AND FACTORS THAT INFLUENCE USE

Intentionality of data design and visualization is critical to development of useful reports. Simon's (2014) assertion that "ignoring or dismissing UX [user experience] will almost certainly result in failure" (p. 95) is not an overstatement. As report developers well know, user experience often determines data usability and frequency of consumption. A good user experience makes interacting with data not only informative, but also enjoyable. Conversely, a poor user experience makes interacting with data a painful endeavor, to be avoided at all cost.

What factors result in a good user experience and encourage use of data for decision-making? First and foremost, reports should be conceived not as a static response to a singular question, but rather as a contextual means of exploration of the broader topic. Consider exploration of a university's IPEDS first-time-in-college institutional retention rate; while it may be minimally sufficient to provide only the current figure, a better approach would be to provide institutional and national trends for context. Good user experience should similarly allow the data to tell the story—not just a fragment of it. Intentional data structures and visualizations are a means of telling the institution's data story (see Figure 10.1).

Second, to develop data reports that tell appropriate stories and ensure a good user experience, we must first consider existing user expectations. Despite

- Reports should explore a topic rather than focus on a single question
- Understanding user expectation is critical to creating usable data
- Good user experience fosters data use
- Data should meet technological expectations of users
- Technological advances, such as interactive data visualization, engage users

FIGURE 10.1 Key Considerations in User Experience.

different roles and needs, there are key commonalities shared by campus data users regarding expectations for data reports. Due to constant technological advances and instant availability of information, users have little interest in traditional static reports. Users expect more interactive functionality to be able to tailor information to their immediate needs. In this respect, fostering momentum is a critical means in engaging users with data. Traditional two-dimensional reports are constrained by the inability to provide an instantaneous exploration of follow-up questions prompted by a report's contents. Resulting questions are noted, put back into the analysis queue, and brought back to the data consumer weeks later for follow-up. This process recurs until all questions have been addressed, or, more likely, the user loses interest in the data due to the prolonged time-frame necessary for analysis.

Third, providing users with data formats that do not meet their technological expectations creates a disconnect and implies to consumers that data are not advanced or timely enough to be relevant to current discussions. To put this into context, consider expectations of current users regarding traditional road maps. Road maps contain the same information as ever and are practical in many situations, however, many users would balk if they were handed one. With the introduction of GPS, the static road map format no longer meets expectations of many users. Road maps require far more interpretation and time to use— users must be able to determine their current direction, where they wish to go, and select the route that appears most appropriate. In contrast, GPS users need only know where they want to go in general; technology does the rest of the work for them. GPS itself is an interactive visualization; it provides immediate and intuitive results in a visually engaging manner. Further, ease of use ensures users do not have to invest ample time to get results they need. This should be the case for good data user experience—users should only need to know where they want to go/what they want to know. Good data structures should facilitate navigation to a response as simply as GPS to a destination.

Fourth, technological advances now allow data stewards to come to the table with active data rather than passive printed reports; this changes not only the way data is shared, but also provides the ability to explore questions arising from data in real time. Building on the benefits of real-time data exploration, the next substantial advancement in data usability comes from integration of data visualization in reports. Data visualization allows for the conveyance of a huge amount of information in a way that does not seem overwhelming. Visualized reporting further enables users to accelerate the process of recognizing trends within the data and responding to complex questions that have historically been delayed due to the lack of an interactive platform.

Yuk and Diamond (2014) suggested a key advantage of visualization is the ability to quickly identify patterns within the data that would not be apparent in static formats. Applying this concept to the current higher education climate, consider the inherent complexity of questions regarding the value and cost of higher education, outcomes, and postgraduate outcomes. In response to associated federal accountability requirements, every Title IV funded institution is required by the Department of Education to disclose its annual retention and graduation outcomes. Dissemination of these data often stimulate additional questions from key stakeholders, not only about the overall retention or graduation rate of an institution, but also about the rates for specific student populations.

Consider how the scope and depth of such data have been displayed historically in static reports; a retention report broken down by program and aggregate demographics in most instances would easily exceed thirty pages. Not only is the lengthy format off-putting, but also users are required to invest time to sift through the pages to locate the data they need. In such an extensive document, something as simple as neglecting to number the pages or failing to include table headers on each page is sufficient to stifle the user experience and prevent the stakeholder from leveraging the data to address their questions. In contrast, the same information, presented as a visualization, fits onto a single interactive page, with the added benefit of allowing users to control data exploration to answer varied questions. This encourages a good user experience and repeated use of the data.

Visualizing data allows data developers to meet consumers at a common point of expectation, fostering data use. Users provided with the opportunity to explore data in real time, based on their own questions, are far more likely to become recurring data users. Making data visually engaging not only facilitates learning, but also minimizes the hesitancy which often accompanies data interpretation. A good visualization provides users with necessary context and clarity to feel comfortable in using data. Data developers have few opportunities to win over data consumers; intentional and targeted data structures are critical to fostering adoption and long-term use of data.

DEVELOPING VISUALIZED DATA

It is important to note that development of visualized and engaging data reports can often be accomplished without devotion of additional financial resources. Reports which encourage user engagement are not contingent upon a particular software platform. As Patil and Mason (2015) noted, "The secret of great data science is that the tools are almost irrelevant" (p. 19). Effective reports can be constructed in almost any software platform, as long as they are developed with intentionality and understanding of user expectations and experience. Engaging interactive dashboards can be created using only Microsoft Excel (see Alexander and Walkenbach's *Microsoft Excel Dashboards & Reports* [2013] and Goldmeier and Duggirala's *Dashboards for Excel* [2015]) or using dedicated visualization software such as Power BI or Tableau. It is not the medium which is important, but rather the story that is told. Data are most usable when they are able to tell a clear and engaging story in response to a user prompt. Consider Figures 10.2 and Figure 10.3. Both address the question: "What are the institutional enrollment trends for the last five years?" in very similar ways using different tools.

As shown by these examples, regardless of the platform or tool, usable data rely on the following commonalities: 1) simplicity, 2) clarity, and 3) intuitive structuring. A data structure which encourages exploration of data can be attained through interactive visualizations or a series of deeper-dive graphs; both methods provide users with a starting point which allows for further exploration. Users have the ability to address the original question, as well as explore deeper and more complex questions all within one visualization. Leveraging data available in the two examples, end users can quickly conclude that there

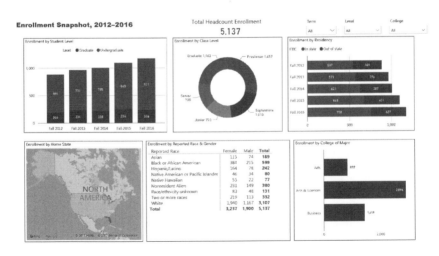

FIGURE 10.2 Enrollment Dashboard in Power BI.

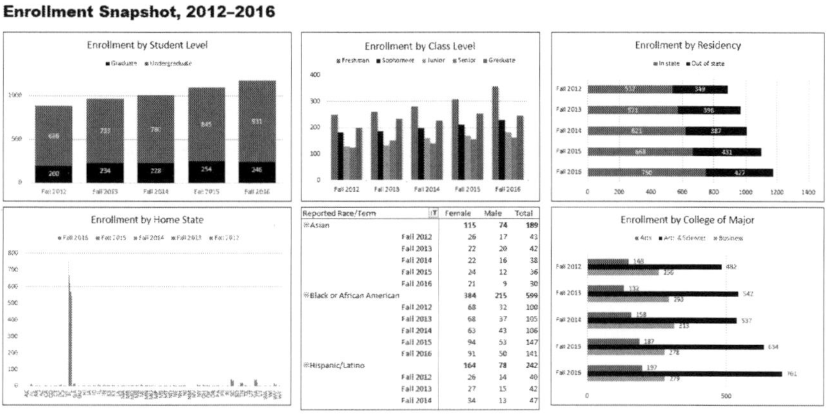

Enrollment Snapshot, 2012–2016

FIGURE 10.3 Enrollment Dashboard in Excel.

has been a positive trend of increased enrollment over the past five years. Based upon this understanding, users can quickly move to deeper questions exploring trends in in-state versus out of state enrollment, enrollment by ethnicity, and college enrollment by major. As such, visualization designed to anticipate follow-up questions and foster a good user experience has the ability to accelerate learning for individuals and the organization. Closing the loop with the GPS metaphor, we must keep in mind that different users rely on the same technology to seek different destinations. In higher education, this is particularly true.

DIFFERENT AUDIENCES, DIFFERENT NEEDS

Awareness of the data needs of the intended audience is critical to encouraging data use. Within higher education, primary data users can be broadly grouped into administrators, faculty, and consumers (prospective students, parents, etc.). Consideration of differing audience needs is critical in the development of usable data reports. Failure to do so results not only in lack of use, but also in the perception that reports and data are designed to favor a particular segment of the institution. Individuals across all audiences have relied on intuition and their "gut" instincts to derive key decisions that impact the institution in the absence of usable and reliable data. As such, development of reports intentionally designed to accommodate the needs of different audiences is critical to foster a data-informed culture. In order to develop effective reports, we must first consider how data needs differ across the three main constituent groups.

Administrators are key data consumers within higher education institutions, especially in institutions that utilize a data-informed decision-making approach. Administrators, individuals tasked with leading departments, colleges, divisions,

131

or institutions have copious data needs and little time. These data users do not have time to guess what the data are saying; content and meaning must be understandable immediately. Clarity hinges on the ability to grasp the *meaning* of the data and the story they tell. In some instances, administrators responsible for making key decisions have limited experience leveraging institutional data to drive key decisions. Administrators are often groomed from the faculty ranks after successfully navigating the tenure-track process—a process which rewards individuals for having a depth of knowledge on a narrow focus of information. The transition from faculty to the administrative ranks requires a shift in the understanding and contextualization of data.

Meaning and understanding of data are grounded in context. Administrators often have a breadth of understanding around key metrics of the institution, but lack the expertise and depth of understanding of key data metrics to drive systemic change. Specifically, they often need guidance and contextualized understanding of in-depth key metrics and data points to facilitate change at the institution. To drive and implement a data-informed culture, these users require multiple years of data in order to understand the bigger picture and impacts of data; point-in-time snapshots are not useful for decision-making. Particularly for administrator level users, a differentiation must be made between actionable data reports and data snapshots.

Snapshots are valuable to administrators as they allow them to provide quick soundbites on key metrics, such as reporting fall enrollment figures in a press release. This is the purpose of snapshot data: to answer a single question as of a single point in time. They are not designed to inform decision-making at a deeper level and should not be used as such. In some cases, the historical reliance on reporting-style snapshot data creates a disconnect with the deeper data needed by administrators. In such cases, data providers don't comprehend the depth or scope of administrator data needs. This problem is exacerbated by the use of differing terminology between administrators and data providers, resulting in a barrier to administrators receiving the information they want in a timely manner. Such barriers result in wasted employee resources and delayed or uninformed decision-making as administrators either request clarification in the form of additional data or move ahead based on an incomplete understanding of existing data. Administrators are often called upon to make rapid decisions with the potential to impact the entire institution; they need to be able to explore relevant data immediately rather than requesting additional data that may, or may not, address the question at hand.

Data needs of *faculty* members tend to be more narrow in scope than those of administrators due to the different nature of their positions and responsibilities. Whereas administrators require broad contextual data to understand the big picture story, faculty members require similar, but more focused, data. The ability for in-depth data exploration remains, however, the focus sharpens as faculty seek to gain insight on their specific programs, courses, or students. Institution-level data becomes critical not for the ability to examine institutional trends, but rather for context of understanding how the program or course data are situated.

Users, especially faculty members, may be resistant to using reports advocated by the administration. One way to minimize this issue is to be intentional about faculty report design. Data myths and hot topics exist on every campus; creating reports around these issues can help draw users to the data. In our experiences, not only has this approach been helpful in encouraging data usage, but has also helped to dispel a number of long-held campus myths. Allowing users to see the truth for themselves through interactive data exploration has proven far more effective than simply presenting data to the contrary. Another key element in attaining faculty use is transparency. The presence of comparison data is a strong motivator for use, as faculty are eager to see how they fare compared to other departments on metrics provided in the report.

External consumers (prospective students, parents, alumni, etc.) use data less frequently and require more detailed guidance to appropriately interpret data. Users in this group include individuals with an interest in higher education data, but not at the same depth as administrators or faculty. This might include prospective students looking for enrollment data to find out about institutional demographics, parents of prospective students looking for graduation rates, or local residents curious about institutional growth over time. Such users are largely unfamiliar with jargon used within higher education and are unaware of commonly used definitions. Reports geared toward informing this group should be carefully designed to ensure all items are clearly defined, use of acronyms is avoided, and data structures are intuitive.

Table 10.1 below summarizes considerations in report development for each of the audience groups discussed in this section.

ONE TOPIC, DIFFERENT AUDIENCES

Despite a shared understanding of the importance of a single topic, a single one-size report fails to provide the scope of detail required by different audiences. To illustrate the data needs of these different higher education audiences, the following section uses the topic of first-to-second year retention to examine how frameworks and contextual needs within a single topic can vary per user type.

Retention Data for Administrators

The majority of institutional administrators on any given campus are able to recite the institution's first-to-second year retention rate at a moment's notice.

Table 10.1 Summary of Audience Values and Needs

Audience	Reports should	Reports should not	Example
Administrators	■ Provide meaning/context ■ Be clear and easy to interpret ■ Provide access to in-depth data on critical data points	■ Focus on a single point in time (snapshot) ■ Require follow-up reports to address common questions	■ Retention trends not only by standard demographics of gender and ethnicity, but by metrics with the potential to inform decision-making on policies, tuition, and aid offered
Faculty	■ Be relevant to specific courses and students ■ Be transparent ■ Address hot topics/faculty concerns	■ Focus on goals perceived to be administrator-driven ■ Contain excessive data jargon without explanation	■ Retention trends within program; specific retention risk information related to their students
Prospective Students, Parents, Alumni, Public	■ Be free of jargon and provide clear definitions ■ Include fewer drill-down visuals and more tables which are less susceptible to misinterpretation ■ Be prominently located	■ Be complex ■ Require advance knowledge of higher education practices or definitions	■ Retention disclosures for prospective students

As a key performance metric for many institutions, this figure is generally well known across campus. As such, a snapshot of historical retention rates is of little or no use to administrators. Deeper data is needed to inform institutional and curricular planning. Rather than data snapshots, administrators find value in hierarchical visualizations which allow instant examination of retention trends, not only by standard demographics of gender and ethnicity, but also by metrics with the potential to inform decision-making on policies, tuition, and aid offered. The ability for users to explore retention trends for majors within a college or specific major reinforces the notion that retention is everyone's responsibility. This approach encourages data usage, as users are able to start with the familiar institutional retention rate and drill down to examine college and major retention rates, with ability to further filter on student demographics. Data are no longer static figures on a page, but dynamic visuals nimble enough to answer program-level questions instantly.

Retention Data for Faculty

Given administrators' focus on the importance of retention and the message of retention as everyone's responsibility, faculty members are often encouraged to take ownership of helping improve retention. At this level, faculty members are interested in data which inform them as to how they might best devote their time and resources to improving programmatic retention. Overall, institutional retention trends are not beneficial to helping faculty make advances in retention; they need specific retention and retention risk information related to their students. Provided this level of data, retention ceases to be an insurmountable institutional concern and becomes an opportunity for a faculty member to interact with a single student.

Retention Data for Prospective Students, Parents, and Public

Data designed for consumers outside of higher education must take into consideration the lack of familiarity with postsecondary terminology and structures. Although the concept of retention is commonplace within higher education, it is likely an unfamiliar one to prospective students and the public. In fact, retention in K-12 education has a negative meaning (to be held back), whereas retention in higher education has a positive meaning (moving forward). As such, reports developed for this audience must provide high levels of clarification and avoid the use of jargon. Information on what retention is, how it is calculated, and why it is important are all necessary to provide contextual understanding of the concept. Distinctions must be made clear that retention relies on federal methodology, which includes only first-time, full-time, degree-seeking college students in the calculation. Consumers may be interested in examining how students within different populations, colleges, and majors fared in comparison to overall institutional rates. Visualized report development not only offers the ability to improve user experience but also the ability to stimulate learning—specifically, as in the retention example of a well-constructed design that stimulates learning facilitated through an enhanced user experience.

IMPACT OF PRACTICAL AND ENGAGING DATA

With attention to user expectations and intentionality of data reports, we seek to increase not only use of data, but also the deeper understanding of data necessary for a successful data-informed culture. Key to encouraging data comprehension is the provision of visualized data reports, which provide a framework for institutional cognitive development and facilitate the efficacy of data dissemination through descriptive, diagnostic, and decision-making context. Simply stated, visualized reports are key to understanding the most salient questions and the data most critical for understanding and providing context for those questions. The impact of effective data visualizations on users can be contextualized through the lens of Bloom's taxonomy. Specifically, visualized reports viewed through the lens of Bloom's taxonomy provide the framework for how well-constructed visualized data facilitate multifaceted hierarchical learning for the end user. When the key stakeholders are first introduced to visualized data, it often sparks in them the ability to recall things they have previously learned.

The foundational component of the Bloom's model of learning is the ability of the learner to identify, list, and recall information. Well-constructed visualized data allow the end users to associate data to information previously conceptualized. This level is the lowest level of learning in the cognitive domain in Bloom's and typically does not bring about a change in behavior, but it is foundational. Learners absorb, remember, recognize, and recall information to make meaningful connections that will allow them to ascend to the more complex components of learning. Remembering is facilitated by engaging visualized reports, which resonate with consumers in a way previous data, historically presented in multiple static reports, could not.

Understanding of data in a robust data climate is multi-layered and multifaceted; mastery of this phase within the current milieu of data is often derailed by the lack of an engaging dissemination solution capable of addressing critical tiered foundational questions. Hierarchical data visualizations, aligned with institutional context, allow users to quickly grasp the structure and meaning of the data. As in level two of Bloom's taxonomy, the initial hierarchical view, at the broadest level, provides a foundation for comprehension and understanding of the data. In traditional static data reports, this is where user development stops, as comprehension of a single fact is often the goal of the report. Hierarchical data visualizations afford users the opportunity to progress deeper into the data, through the application of personal knowledge to interact with the data in more meaningful ways. This level of individualized exploration allows users to discover and control data in ways that are applicable to their unique situations. As Ware (2012) noted, "a good visualization is something that allows us to drill down and find more data about anything that seems important" (p. 345). Interactive data visualization facilitates the ability of the end users to contextualize their understanding and comprehend crucial foundational concepts, fostering a shift from merely asking questions to leveraging appropriate data and insight to identify underlying assumptions. This process, as articulated by Ware (2012), results in level three of Bloom's taxonomy. Most importantly, the application of visualized data enhances the learning of the individual in regards to identifying and selecting appropriate resources to leverage data needed to solve critical questions.

Hierarchical visualization facilitates this ability for users to apply knowledge to institutional data by identifying and exploring data through the lens of their experiences. It is at this stage that hierarchical visualization promotes development of higher order skills of analysis and synthesis. Analysis springs from exploration of data, as it is through interaction with the data that users make connections and gain insight. The intentionally designed visualized report provides the venue for users to not just recall, describe, or interpret data, but also to build on these foundational components to leverage data for meaning making. Data are not simply understood and contextualized in their current state; they are used to draw connections, leverage appropriate data, and articulate underlying assumptions. The levels of interactivity and exploration necessary to promote data analysis and synthesis are not offered by traditional static reports, thus halting user momentum and development. Recalling the retention example presented earlier in the chapter, the ability to move from drawing connections between historical retention patterns of various ethnic groups within targeted majors to proposing solutions for increasing retention with these targeted groups is often delayed or never leveraged because the data are present in antiquated tables and charts. Data insights are often buried so deeply in static reports that users lose the ability to leverage the data to construct and design solutions. In comparison, hierarchical data visualizations construct for users the opportunity to progress deeper into the data through a series of interactive clicks within a single page. This process accelerates learning as lower order questions are quickly answered and users are able to build on understanding to focus on ideas and solutions that are truly data-informed. Visualization allows a department chair to identify and act on previously unknown patterns within his/her majors and to compare those patterns to those of other majors across the university for additional context.

Further, due to the limited scope of data presented within static reports, users might draw conclusions based upon historical myths and misconceptions to fill in the gaps. Well-designed and defined visual reports allow the data to tell a more complete story, which facilitates pathways for data-derived judgments that are evidence based. These data allow stakeholders to cultivate an environment that shifts organizational culture from decision-making based upon historical myths and misconceptions to an environment that is data-informed. Accessible and usable data encourage users to draw conclusions from data and act upon them. For example, the chair of the chemistry department can assess the success rates of organic chemistry; the data can be disaggregated by course grade, gender, ethnicity, and class times. Hierarchical visualization facilitates the ability for the chair to create interventions based on patterns identified within the data, such as a gap in the success rates for individuals who receive an A in a particular course versus those who get a B—or lower. Data can further be leveraged to determine if there is a pattern related to success rates and sequencing of prerequisite courses. Accessible data allow the chair to engage with the data, identify patterns, and conclude that the department needs to leverage a course redesign to improve the success rates.

COMMON PITFALLS AND CONSIDERATIONS

To increase awareness of issues that render reports difficult to use, a series of commonly occurring pitfalls impacting data usability are provided below, along with guidance on ways to avoid such issues in development of effective data reports.

- Pitfall: Failing to consider user expectations
  Consider: Would a user find the data engaging and intuitive? Is the report too extensive/lengthy/detailed? How would you react if you received the report?
- Pitfall: Expecting users to understand complex data
  Consider: Examine data from an outsider perspective—what needs additional clarification? Are all the data elements necessary? Can the report be simplified?
- Pitfall: Losing user momentum/interest
  Consider: What are likely follow-up questions to stem from the data? Maintain user momentum by anticipating and addressing follow-up questions.
- Pitfall: Developing one-size-fits-all reports
  Consider: Different users have different foci and different questions of the same data. Does developing a single report result in loss of depth necessary for users?
- Pitfall: Creating bad visualizations (too much on the page, clashing colors, etc.)
  Consider: "As a data visualization newbie, your focus should be on building intelligent data visualizations with actionable data. The data visualization should have a clear story that the audience can identify. Therefore, focusing on audiences with similar needs is important" (Yuk & Diamond, 2014, p. 193).
- Pitfall: Ignoring campus data myths
  Consider: As an ongoing topic of interest, myths are a way to draw users to the data. Providing visualized and exploratory data on these areas can help dispel myths. Users are more likely to accept data they can interact

with and explore—it adds a level of transparency and ownership (the difference between "I saw it myself" and "the administration told me so.")

■ Pitfall: Developing engaging visuals for every request
Consider: Sometimes a simple table will suffice; weigh the time investment and need for the data. Don't make things more complex than they need to be.

PRACTICAL SUGGESTIONS AND GUIDANCE

As we have noted throughout, the key to developing usable data is intentionality and consideration of the end user experience. Too often reports are created and shared without consideration of context, related questions, or design. The following suggestions provide a framework for consideration in the development of practical and engaging data reports.

■ *Anticipate follow-up questions.* Ask yourself, what is the logical next question to the story that the data tells? Add this piece to your report and repeat the process until the report tells the full story.

■ *Avoid data overload.* Realize that end users who are not data lovers have a low saturation point; put the most important points first and ensure the report does not look overwhelming.

■ *Ensure data tell a complete story.* Knaflic (2015) suggests storyboarding your data before creating a report to increase intentionality of the final product. Begin with your key issue or question and work toward ending with a single sentence of the overall story conveyed by the data.

■ *Promote clarity.* Include a section which provides definitions, sources, a sample data interpretation, navigation tips, and developer contact information. This helps to minimize the occurrence of misinterpretation by users.

■ *Create strategic data visualizations.* Keep user experience in mind. Don't try to fit everything on a single page; take advantage of drill-down features to provide layers of data without cluttering the page. Consider providing detailed information on additional pages so users can view it, if they desire to do so.

■ *Use your campus mythology.* Rely on common campus misunderstandings and hot topic issues to draw users to reports. Every institution has them; making the data available will draw in users that might not otherwise explore the data.

■ *Embrace branding.* Use institutional colors and logos on all reports; this encourages the understanding reports are legitimate and sanctioned institutional documents.

SUMMARY

As higher education practitioners, we are bombarded with data reports on a daily basis. And who among us can profess to truly reading each and every report that finds its way onto our desks or into our inboxes? The increase in data availability has resulted in more and more users developing reports, many of which will go unread, resulting in a waste of time and resources. It is our hope that with an increased awareness of the value of intentionality and user experience, greater consideration will be given to the development of reports that can truly be used to cultivate a data culture.

DISCUSSION QUESTIONS

1. What factors encourage you to explore or dive deeper into a data report? What factors discourage you? Can you share these concepts with the data report creators?
2. What are your own expectations in relation to data reports? How often are they met? If your expectations are not met, can you pinpoint why?
3. What tools available at your institution might be harnessed to develop usable reports?
4. What topics might be of high interest and engage users at your institution in data use?
5. Which reports at your institution contain good information but are not given much attention? What factors contribute to this perception? How might the reports be revised to improve usability?
6. Consider constituents on your campus who are data averse—how might you develop or revise reports to appeal to those users?

REFERENCES

Bock, L. (2015). Introduction. In C. N. Knaflic, *Storytelling with data: A data visualization guide for business professionals* (pp. ix–x). Hoboken, NJ: John Wiley & Sons.

Duggirala, P. (2015). *Dashboards for Excel*. Berkeley, CA: Apress.

Knaflic, C. N. (2015). *Storytelling with data: A data visualization guide for business professionals* (1st ed.) Hoboken, NJ: John Wiley & Sons.

Patil, D. & Mason, H. (2015). *Data-Informed: Creating a data culture*. Sebastopol, CA: O'Reilly. Retrieved from www.oreilly.com/data/free/data-informed.csp.

Simon, P. (2014). *The visual organization: Data visualization, big data, and the quest for better decisions*. Hoboken, NJ: John Wiley & Sons.

Walkenbach, J. (2013). *Excel dashboards and reports* (2nd ed.). Hoboken, NJ: Wiley & Sons.

Ware, C. (2012). *Interactive technologies: Information visualization: Perception for design* (3rd ed.). Burlington, MA: Morgan Kaufmann.

Yuk, M. & Diamond, S. (2014). *Data visualization for dummies*. Hoboken, NJ: John Wiley & Sons.

Chapter 11

Communicating and Disseminating Data

Wendy Kallina

INTRODUCTION

With so many data tools readily available, it might seem that embedding data within the institutional culture is simply a matter of choosing and implementing the right tool or suite of tools. This approach to data dissemination and usage often ends with a list of discarded "solutions" and an unhealthy (but perhaps merited) skepticism about being able to access data and make progress toward creating a data-informed decision process. Too often, the demand is on the consumer to learn a software tool as well as to become fluent in the language of research, statistics, or analytics. Instead, the demand should be on analysts to frame results and insights within the context of the institution. Some consumers, given tools appropriate to their time constraints and interests, will have the knowledge and background to transform their data into usable information. Other consumers may find themselves at a disadvantage in a system that may be data-rich but is not user-friendly. As discussed in Chapter 10, finding a way to meet the needs of most consumers is the surest way to advance data use, improve communication, and facilitate trust in both the data and the process.

This chapter focuses on factors affecting data communication. These factors include knowing the audience, determining what to share, and communicating and sharing effectively.

KNOWING YOUR AUDIENCE

Understanding the organizational structure of an institution is important when considering how to effectively communicate with the audience. The institutional research (IR) office is the home of much of the institutional data, although there are other units (e.g., student affairs, alumni) who house their own unit-specific data. The location of the IR office, with the majority located in

Academic Affairs or the Office of the President, leads to what Swing and Ross (2016) describe as a "ranked set of users." The president, chief academic officer, and mandatory reporting requirements are ranked first and consume the majority of the office's resources. After these high-priority clients are served, the remaining resources are then divided among the lower-priority clients—a situation that can result in limited access to data and analytic services for these consumers.

The unit data outside of IR office may be shared and used within the department for specific tasks and goals but may not be shared with other departments. In these cases, it is typically not a lack of resources that hinders dissemination and use, but a limited understanding of why the unit-specific data would be of interest to other departments or audiences. Data silos can occur when data systems are not integrated, but silos persist when consumers do not recognize how data may be used outside of its original purpose. For example, a student affairs office collects attendance data for events and extracurricular organizations. These data are used within student affairs for determining the popularity of events and planning for future events. Academic affairs is interested in these data as an indicator of student engagement, and IR can combine the student affairs data with student engagement survey data or student satisfaction data to explore the associations between observed student behavior (i.e., event attendance) and self-reported student behaviors or attitudes. If student major is added as a variable to the student affair data, the alumni office or foundation office can reach out to alumni in those majors as sponsors or attendees for future events. The investment, including time and money, in the data is maximized as the data are used by multiple consumers. Data silos limit data use and restrict potential audiences.

Differences in access and responsiveness, along with data silos, make it difficult to assess the institutional culture and audience expectations surrounding data. Consumers have different experiences based on the amount of data they know about and have access to, as well as their knowledge of and access to individuals who can transform the data. Even when shared, consumers who have received data and information without attention to their specific needs as the target audience may find it incomprehensible or simply unusable. There is no "one-size-fits-all" report—a report should be tailored, when possible, to its intended audience.

President, Provosts, and other Executives

The audience, comprising the president, provost, or other senior staff, expects the skilled researcher to demonstrate an understanding of the interest, issue, or problem being examined and to tailor the results accordingly. This audience is the most likely to have access to institutional dashboards or reports on key

143

performance indicators (KPIs). Members of this audience are the least likely to have the time to run reports, much less to fully engage in extensive analysis to arrive at their own insights.

Administrators

Administrators may include associate/assistant vice-presidents, deans, chairs, and other unit heads. Their scope of responsibilities is more limited than the executive group. As noted in Chapter 10, with this narrower scope comes the demand for more data depth. Elaborate customized data and reporting systems may support specific information needs for the unit. Some of these administrators are the expert in their units and are very knowledgeable about theory, data sources, and common KPIs specific to unit function. There may be specific benchmarks that can be compared to other institutions. However, if there is not a culture of broad data dissemination and transparency, administrators may not have comparison points within the institution. For example, customized grade distribution reports could be created for individual departments. By using the reports, a department chair may know the average DFW rate (i.e., the number of grades of D, F, or W in a course) for general education courses taught in the department but may not know how this rate compares to general education courses for the institution.

Members of this audience are likely to have access to a data and reporting system housed in the unit, or role-based access to unit specific data and reports in an enterprise system. Due to their position in the institution, administrators may be interested in developing a deeper understanding of their own data, gaining a greater understanding of how their information compares to other units, or seeing their contributions to the larger institutional picture. Interested in both depth and a broader context, this audience may want to drill down into the data, while simultaneously discussing how departmental goals contribute to the institution's strategic plan.

Faculty

Faculty members are another potential audience. A common assumption is that consumers with a graduate degree are already proficient in analyzing and interpreting data. However, research within a discipline does not automatically transfer to research proficiency in higher education. As with any discipline, IR and assessment have their own theories, bodies of literature, assumptions, and practices. Faculty members are likely to question the methodology and ask to examine the data or analyses for themselves. This is not surprising as academics are trained to propose, defend, review, and revise. Even collaboration is hierarchical as evidenced by the order of authorship for publications. Similar to administrators, faculty members are most likely to hone in on data and results that are relevant to their interests.

Support Staff

Support staff includes individuals who enter data into institutional systems and those who may retrieve it in the form of reports for the unit, faculty, administrators, or executives. This audience often receives in-house training on how to utilize tools or systems, and are responsible for generating the majority of reports. Despite being the group that is most likely to retrieve data and reports, they are the least likely to have formal training in data management, data analysis, or data presentation. Support staff often have limited exposure to how data are transformed into usable information for evaluation and planning.

Students

Students report their personal, financial, prior academic, testing, health, and attitudinal and behavioral data to institutions in the forms of applications, required paperwork, and student surveys. Communication with students and their parents may include institutional data such as enrollment, retention, and graduation rates included in admission materials or available on sites such as College Navigator (https://nces.ed.gov/collegenavigator). Despite collecting large amounts of data from students, the information flow back to students is notoriously weak. Sharing results and providing students with information as to how their data are being used is part of creating an institutional culture of transparency and collaboration. The NSSE Institute promotes communicating the results and actions taken based on data to multiple consumers, including students (http://nsse.indiana.edu/html/sharing_NSSE_results.cfm).

DETERMINING WHAT TO SHARE TO WHOM

Data and information move through an organization by being shared in both formal and informal settings. Organizational norms on data-sharing and data literacy affect what is shared and with whom it is shared. Returning to the previous DFW example, there are institutions that publish grade distributions on their website with options to filter by course and instructor. This information is not gated and is available to members of the institution as well as to the general public. Only courses with insufficient enrollment to adequately protect identification of students are omitted. Other institutions make the information available to senior administrators with data aggregated by course, course acronym, department, or college so that individual courses and faculty are not identified. Still others make grade distributions disaggregated by course and faculty member available to administrators but only to be shared within the department with the faculty member. Sharing grade distributions with the instructor, perhaps as formative or summative feedback by the department head, is clearly a formal setting that supports limited sharing and data use. The availability of grade distributions on an institution's website supports both formal sharing and use but also informal sharing of data across multiple contexts and stakeholders (e.g., students, full-time and part-time faculty, staff, administrators, board members, affiliated organizations, and parents).

CREATING A CULTURE OF SHARING

At every institution, there are files—paper and electronic—filled with data that could have been utilized when they were fresh and newly collected. Instead, they were stored until someone considered knowledgeable enough to do the analysis could be found, or until the acknowledged experts could find the time to do the analysis. There may have been fear that the data would somehow be handled and analyzed incorrectly with disastrous results. There may have been concerns about sensitive information being released with no clearly designated process for ensuring data security.

A more troubling, but not unknown, reason for withholding data and information that might be gained from it, is the belief that its release would result in the loss of power for some group or individual. To remain a base of power, information must be withheld in circumstances where it could be relevant. Once the information is disclosed or the relevant situation passes, the power is gone. Consider the administration of an employee satisfaction survey. Data can be disaggregated by department and position (e.g., staff, faculty, administrator). Results reveal no differences by position but there are significant differences in satisfaction between departments. The resulting report focuses on the overall high satisfaction of employees regardless of position. The departmental differences are not shared per the study's sponsor's request. The sponsor's home department is one of the departments with the lowest satisfaction scores. The sponsor, by withholding data to protect the department and perhaps their own standing in the department, may actually have prevented the department from receiving resources to better understand and address the issue. To create a data-sharing culture, the benefits of sharing must outweigh the temporary power or rewards that withholding data may provide.

Another sharing situation is being played out among researchers, many of whom must make their data available as part of receiving federal funding. In this context, data-sharing includes providing raw data through data repositories, websites, or directly upon request. Researchers are concerned with how "their data" may be used, and with the loss of potential publications to other researchers who pose similar questions. These concerns are not supported in the literature. Data-sharing, both formally and informally, was associated with increases in publication metrics including primary investigator publications (Pienta, Alter, & Lyle, 2010). Among social scientists and STEM researchers, data-sharing behaviors were associated with perceived career benefit and perceived normative pressure (Kim & Adler, 2015; Kim & Zhang, 2015). Believing that data-sharing is personally advantageous and is an expected behavior are related to data-sharing behavior.

For an institution to create a culture of data-sharing, the definition for data-sharing success could include the extent of data and information that are disseminated to, and then used by, consumers and stakeholders rather than the absolute number of reports generated by an office. Using data has a very different set of expectations and outcomes that goes beyond the creation of data reports. For an end user, a data report is similar to entering a zip code into a weather app and getting the forecast. If the forecast calls for rain, there are multiple decisions to make depending on why the data were retrieved. A raincoat? Rain boots? An umbrella? Adjust the sprinkler system? These are all decisions that may be driving the reason to retrieve weather data. The successful installation of the app is a technical task. If people are racing through the rain, in their good shoes, without an umbrella, seeking to find the shortest path to their destination without running through the sprinklers—when the forecast was 100% chance of rain—it is not the data tool or data that is the problem, but rather data retrieval and use.

The ease of using technology to retrieve many types of data has contributed to a "self-service" approach in the way that data are accessed by consumers. Gartner (2017) defines self-service analytics "as a form of business intelligence in which line-of-business professionals are enabled and encouraged to perform queries and generate reports on their own, with nominal IT support." Although self-service analytic platforms contribute to the democratization of the data in terms of access, access does not create a culture of sharing. Generating reports does not make the user any more expert in how to use data and formulate questions. This "self-service" approach, by itself, does not improve the data literacy of consumers or the institution.

DATA LITERACY

Data use and interactions around data are largely affected by the data literacy of individuals who make up the organizational unit. Searches for the term "data literacy" yield multiple books and articles for teachers and librarians but surprisingly few sources for higher education. This emphasis on K-12 may be the unintended consequence of the No Child Left Behind Act of 2001 and its emphasis on standards and measurement. The Data Quality Campaign (DQC), launched in 2005, is a "nonprofit, nonpartisan, national advocacy organization committed to realizing an education system in which all stakeholders—from parents to policymakers—are empowered with high-quality data from the early childhood, K-12, postsecondary, and workforce systems" (2014a, p. 1). As of 2017, the majority of resources posted on the site are related to K-12. The 2014 DQC definition of data-literate educators is as follows:

> Data-literate educators continuously, effectively, and ethically access, interpret, act on, and communicate multiple types of data from state, local, classroom, and other sources to improve outcomes for students in a manner appropriate to educators' professional roles and responsibilities (Data Quality Campaign, 2014b, p. 1).

By replacing "educators" with "higher education professionals" and adding "other stakeholders" to describe stakeholders other than students, we arrive at a definition for data-literate higher educational professionals.

> Data-literate *higher education professionals* continuously, effectively, and ethically access, interpret, act on, and communicate multiple types of data from federal, state, local, classroom, and other sources to improve outcomes for students *and other stakeholders* in a manner appropriate to the *professionals'* roles and responsibilities.

What does it take for a higher educational professional to become data-literate? A common misperception is that data literacy is something that mainly "number" or "data" people possess. Data literacy is not an innate talent for numbers but rather a skill set that higher education professionals can learn and develop as part of their role in the institution. Institutional researchers and other individuals with similar highly developed data literacy skill sets can facilitate this learning. Training on how to choose, access, evaluate, and use data should be targeted to all levels of the organization. The data literacy of an organization is not determined by the data literacy of top executives but rather by the data literacy of everyone who interacts with systems and data as part of their work role.

Certain foundational structures and practices support the development of data literacy. Data are constantly being created from multiple sources. Information about these data sources and data elements should be available and maintained in data dictionaries to decrease the incidence of incorrect entry, use, and interpretation. Ethical, appropriate access and use of data should be supported with clear data governance structures and procedures. Varying levels of expertise in analytical skills are expected, and professionals should be aware of and have resources available should an analysis exceed their current skill level. Creating and supporting the growth of data literacy skills in higher education professionals across an institution can result in more discrimination in choosing data sources, increasingly sophisticated questions and analyses, and more informed discussions.

COMMUNICATING AND SHARING EFFECTIVELY

Candidates for executive or administrative positions can expect interview questions addressing their experience in, and evidence of, making data-informed decisions. Many of today's job descriptions for institutional researchers or analysts emphasize knowledge of data-based planning or decision-support along with the more familiar required analytic and technical skills.

Institutions are seeking individuals who can communicate data to be used for decisions, and seasoned analysts and researchers recognize that this is more than providing a report or presentation to consumers. A prepared presenter understands the characteristics of the anticipated audience and is sensitive to the institutional context discussed in Chapter 3. A presenter can also facilitate the delivery of information through data or empirical storytelling, and by understanding the processes underlying data-informed decision-making.

Storytelling

Data do not tell stories—people do. A book is a story told by the author to the readers. A movie is a story told by a director to the viewers. A presentation is a story told by a speaker to the audience. Although stories can be told through many mediums, the intent is to transmit information with meaning. The information, or topic, is what attracts the reader, viewer, or attendee. The meaning is what keeps them interested and willing to continue to engage in the topic. The data topic may be important to the audience but it is the data story that invites the audience to engage in the creation and use of information.

Stephen Tracy (2016) coined the term "empirical storytelling" to describe the intersection of data science with the art of storytelling. He contends that valuable insights from data can be lost because of poor presentation and a lack of an emotional connection to the audience. Memorable stories resonate with an audience, and empirical storytellers possess the skills to craft the data into a memorable story.

To tell a data story, the storyteller uses both analytical skills and presentation skills in working with the data and the audience. For example, the storyteller uses analytical skills to do a deep dive into the data but presentation skills to describe that dive to different audiences in ways that make sense. To work with multiple audiences, the storyteller must be fluent in different languages and act as an interpreter between groups to facilitate understanding. After describing that deep data dive, the storyteller may then address the implications and application of the information gained from those data to a broader context such as strategic planning. This fluency allows the empirical storyteller to interpret the technical details within the context of the business question. The storyteller develops and increases fluency by collaborating across groups and disciplines, and by participating in conversations and projects.

For institutional researchers, this description of fluency may seem very similar to Terenzini's (1993) description of three different types of organizational intelligence. Technical intelligence comprises basic knowledge and analytical skills. This is the understanding of the data elements and the skills for data use. Issues intelligence is an understanding of the institutional concerns and people associated with those areas of concerns. These are the many audiences or stakeholder groups—all with different languages and viewpoints—who may have competing interests or demands. Contextual intelligence is understanding the broader context or culture of both higher education and one's campus. Effective storytellers are likely to possess all three types of intelligence.

How do storytellers use these skills to construct a story? Storytellers start with a business question, or purpose for the story that is shared by the audience. This is the theme of the story. At the end of the story, the audience should have a greater understanding of why the story needed to be told—the answer to "So what?"—why it matters. The setting, characters, plot, and conflict are the where, who, what, and how details around the theme.

The setting, or where, of a story is the time and place. This is the "Once upon a time, and far, far away" statement. In this instance, it tells the audience that the information is not recent and it did not occur in the current or a nearby location. For a data story, the setting provides a description of when and where the issue originated. The setting is both an introduction and an invitation to the audience to engage in the story as they are provided with contextual and temporal cues. As the story unfolds, the audience should know why the story is being told here and now. What are the politics, policies, institutional challenges, or events that preceded the question?

The characters are the actors in the story. In a data story, data are characters that can be named and described. Participants, instruments, and other measures are all characters in the story. Data are not simply numbers, data represent people, actions, dollars, beliefs, behaviors, etc. The empirical storyteller is able to bring these representations forward so the audience is hearing a story, a memorable story, rather than deciphering a chart or diagram.

The plot is the series of events in the story. Events about data include how they were collected, why they were selected, and how they were analyzed. As the plot unfolds, the audience gains a greater understanding of the underlying question and sources of conflict around the question. The storyteller leads the audience through the analysis strategy and assists the audience in making sense of results. Results can confirm audience expectations, challenge the audience's previous understanding of the issue, or raise new questions. The successful storyteller facilitates the audience's creation and use of information in answering "So what?"

The effectiveness of a storyteller is not measured in "happy endings," where all questions are clearly answered, solutions and next steps are obvious, and consensus about the data and courses of action are reached. A well-told story is one that facilitates or enhances the audience's understanding of the issue, data, analyses, or conclusions. It may be a summary story of a successful project, an informative story about a new issue, or some combination of endings and beginnings. It may reduce conflict surrounding an issue or it may create new conflict. As an institution embraces "data-informed decision-making," the expectation may be that data, especially when presented by an empirical storyteller, will make the decision process easier or quicker. Data are an input to decision-making, not the outcome of decision-making. Few decisions are so clear, so compelling, and without any foreseeable undesirable consequences, that all stakeholders agree.

DATA AND DECISION-MAKING

Even the most carefully crafted story, told by a compelling presenter with pristine data, does not ensure that the decision-making process will go smoothly. The audience may agree with the data and move into a process of decision-making. It is also possible that the data become a point of contention. Honda's Typology of Data and Decision Agreement captures four combinations of data acceptance and decisiveness (Honda, Knight, Kelly, Morimoto, & Coughlin, 2017). The matrix features data analysis on the vertical axis and decision-making on the horizontal axis with "agree" and "disagree" creating a dichotomy for each dimension. Data analysis is defined as the presentation of results including details of the analysis such as sample, size, response rate, and methodology. Decision-making is defined as activities such as generating options, and setting strategies or goals. There are four types or scenarios: Full Consensus, Competing Options, Full Discord, and Anecdotal Decision.

- ■ *Full Consensus.* In Quadrant I, the upper left corner, the audience agrees on both data and decision. If the data were collected to provide additional support for a decision already agreed upon, and the data are as expected, then the audience may arrive at an immediate consensus with very little communication effort from the presenter and little or no deliberation by the audience members.
- ■ *Competing Options.* In Quadrant II, the upper right corner, data are agreed upon but not the decision. The audience could be stakeholders with competing needs when limited resources are available. Additional

data or input may be necessary to move the discussion forward or to rank the desirability of multiple options. Additional data could be creating cost-benefit analyses for selected options, and additional input could be moving the data and options up the chain of command to determine if there is a preferred decision. Competing options does not mean a decision cannot be reached without additional data or input. Stakeholders may simply need additional time to work through data and options to arrive at a full consensus.

- *Full Discord.* In Quadrant III, the lower right corner, there is no agreement on the data or decision. Disagreement about the data could result from differences in theoretical approach, challenges to the methodology (e.g., participant selection, instrument choice), response rates, analysis strategies, or interpretation of results. If given the option, participants may be willing to work through the data, perhaps pulling in other data sources or strategies. Reconciling the data differences could form the foundation for working toward a decision. Disagreement about the data could also be a manifestation of dogmatic beliefs, departmental politics, and other agendas rather than a critique of the data. Disagreeing with the data can also be a strategy to prevent the decision-making process from moving forward.
- *Anecdotal Decision.* In Quadrant IV, the lower left corner, the group may decide not to use the data but arrive at a decision. Although it would appear that the data are rejected, it is likely that other personnel, institutional, environmental, or political data points are informing the decision.

Figure 11.1 shows the typology for data analysis and decision-making. These types illustrate different ways decision makers interact with the data and each other. The typologies are not an unchanging characteristic of the group, but a snapshot taken during the decision-making process. By recognizing what type of process is occurring, an analyst may see opportunities to clarify the data or the communication of the data

Storytelling and Decisions

Honda's typology provides the data storyteller with a framework to assist in determining how the data story is being received and used (Honda et al., 2017). Once the story is told, and the decision-making process has begun, the storyteller as the analyst or with the assistance of an analyst, can assess and anticipate additional or future data and information needs. Although audience members may be familiar with the issue and data, it is unlikely that anyone but the analyst has spent as much time on the data details. The storyteller, in constructing the data story, has placed the data in the context of the business question and

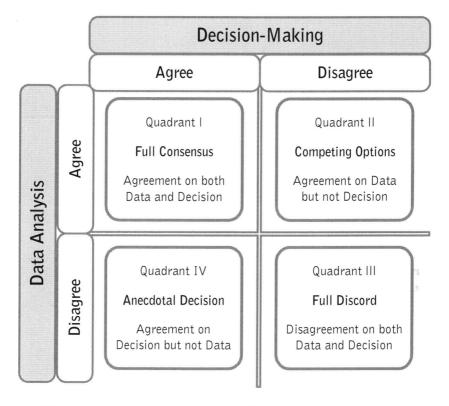

FIGURE 11.1 Typology for Data Analysis and Decision-Making.

becomes a potential resource in the decision-making process. The following examples demonstrate how an empirical storyteller might provide additional data and decision-support.

Example 1. If the audience reaches full consensus (Quadrant I), there may have been clear choices, perhaps previously discussed or agreed upon, associated with specific data outcomes. The audience may give both verbal and non-verbal cues suggesting that the data are understood.

Data story. Co-requisite remediation has been shown to increase student success in gateway courses in math and English. An institution with traditional non-credit developmental courses pilots co-requisite remediation. Pilot data show significant increases in student success in subsequent courses with no increases in institutional costs.

Decision. Implement co-requisite remediation and discontinue developmental courses. Decision is supported by pilot data. Full consensus.

Potential communication strategies. Provide data and decision in summary form that are easily understood and communicated to internal and external stakeholders. Depending on the audience and the directive of the sponsor, this could be an informal summary email or a formal document. The storyteller may communicate the information directly to stakeholders or may provide the information to the sponsor or committee to be included in their communications.

Example 2. If cues indicating agreement with the data are absent, then an immediate consensus on a decision could be an indication of underlying factors or politics that could suppress discussions or dissent, or it could be associated with not understanding the information. The former is symptomatic of an issue outside of the presentation of data; the latter can be gently probed. People want to be viewed by their colleagues as knowledgeable. If there is little substantive discussion or only a few people who appear to be attending to the data, a few clarifying comments about the data and an invitation for questions could be useful.

Data story. A five-year program review shows enrollment numbers and completion rates for a program are decreasing. The graduation rate for the program is increasing. Should the program be continued or discontinued?

Decision. Program to be discontinued. Immediate consensus by some group members.

Potential communication strategies. Clarification regarding how the three metrics are related emphasizing that the graduation rate is based on a subset of students who may only comprise a small percentage of the program.

If the audience responds to clarifying questions with comments or non-verbal cues (e.g., nodding head in agreement, making eye contact) indicating the data were understood and the decision stands, then consensus is confirmed. However, clarification could result in movement to any of the other three types. If it becomes clear that the data were not understood or deemed irrelevant to the decision, and there is no interest in further discussion, then the group has reached an anecdotal decision. If clarification sparks conversation about the quality or relevance of the data, these new understandings could move the group into a full consensus about the data. Given this new information, the stakeholders may decide to re-examine the original decision and possibly explore alternatives. The group has then moved into Quadrant II, Competing Options. Or, clarification may have resulted in both the data and the decision being questioned and the group moving into disagreement with both—Quadrant III, Full Discord.

Example 3. Full discord could also be the starting point for audiences that come in with competing interests. Discussion around points of disagreements regarding the data and resolution could move the group into a discussion of competing options. It is also possible that, given the inability to agree about the data, the group discontinues the data discussion and turns to anecdotal evidence to make decisions.

Data story. Students need timely information regarding their academic progress. Mid-term grades were used in the past with mixed results. Should instructors be required to submit mid-term grades?

Decision 1. Stakeholders point to data that support their position and dismiss conflicting data as flawed. No consensus on data or decision. Full discord.

Potential communication strategies. Acknowledge the mixed results, draw attention to any themes that appear in the data (e.g., success tended to be associated with general education courses, courses that met three times a week had higher instructor response rates), respond to questions.

Decision 2. Stakeholders determine that the "research" is not useful but that they have all encountered students who reported no instructor feedback until well past mid-term. The group agrees that "good" instructors provide feedback often and early, and mid-term grades seem a logical extension of this practice. The stakeholders are now working with anecdotal evidence.

Potential communication strategies. Anecdotal evidence is data. Discarding traditional definitions of validity and reliability, the stakeholders became the anecdotal storytellers and arrived at a consensus. Brainstorming ways to measure the effectiveness of proposed change could refocus the group on empirical data and a discussion on competing options, or it could lead to a measurement strategy for the evaluation of the decision.

SUMMARY

Institutions are complex entities and differences in data access and utilization for decision-making are expected between and within units. Leaders must model the commitment to increased data-sharing and greater data literacy for a cultural change to occur. Stakeholders might not ask questions or make linkages to relevant data or issues, if they are unaccustomed to even receiving data. Employees and other stakeholders increase their data-literacy when data are communicated in a language they understand and when they are given the opportunity to practice data-informed decision-making. Skilled analysts and storytellers serve as an institutional resource and as facilitators to the process.

One major challenge is to accept that decision makers—especially at a senior level—have other constituents affected by decisions being made and stakeholders to whom they are accountable. The decision that appears to not be data-informed but anecdotal, may be informed by less tangible data points related to the larger context (e.g., politics, perceived inequities in resources, reputation, etc.). An empirical analysis and its narrative may not capture the limited resources, competing priorities, differing philosophies, and other factors that contribute to an audience member's interpretation of the story. Put simply, complete transparency in data or in the decision-making process is not always possible—or even desirable in the case of sensitive information.

155

Finally, the creation of new ideas, formation of new insights, or generation of new options does not result from producing more graphs or drilling down into the data. These occur because the data become information created with the audience. Being aware of and tailoring the information to differing levels of data literacy among consumers contributes to the likelihood of arriving at shared understandings about the origins and intent of the data collection, even when there is disagreement about its interpretation and use.

PRACTICAL SUGGESTIONS AND GUIDANCE

In this chapter, audience characteristics were painted with broad strokes. The descriptions were not intended to be applied to individuals but to serve as a starting point for thinking about how stakeholders differ in their data access and use.

- *Understand cultural changes do not happen overnight.* Executive leaders should celebrate collaborative efforts to use data and make maximizing data investments a priority in data governance. Administrators should prepare to work with analysts and other data-literate resource people to educate their units and associated stakeholders about data practices, data sources, and analysis as it pertains to their role. The IR office and other analysts should not overestimate stakeholders' understanding of common data elements (e.g., graduation rates, IPEDS cohorts) or underestimate interest in institutional data and KPIs.
- *Become a storyteller.* Data storytellers and those who want to become data storytellers should continue to develop their analytical and presentation skills. Watching the presentations and reading the documents prepared by others can expand an existing repertoire of skills or provide examples for newer storytellers. TED Talks and other professional productions and tutorials are going to provide a practiced, often scripted, experience, which may translate well in formal settings with selected audiences. YouTube and other amateur resources featuring tutorials or group interaction (e.g., a classroom) can be rich sources of alternate ways to explain an analysis or display information. Either provides the storyteller with the opportunity to adopt the audience perspective. Professional meetings provide opportunities to be the storyteller, and to observe and learn (or not learn) from keynote speakers, seasoned presenters, and colleagues.

DISCUSSION QUESTIONS

1. Are the descriptions of the different audiences consistent with your experience? What additional information would be helpful to know about audiences at your institution?

2. What is the institution's culture of data-sharing? Are there any formal statements or commitments to data-sharing? Where might these statements be appropriate?

3. What units in your institution are data-literate? How do you know? What lessons can be learned from these units?

4. How does one become fluent in the language of multiple stakeholders—what kind of education and experience are necessary?

5. What factors affect decision makers? How do we reconcile decisions when the "data" don't seem to support them?

6. Are sophisticated visualizations necessary to tell a data story?

7. What opportunities are available at your institution to learn and develop technical, analytical, presentation, or storytelling skills?

8. Do you have empirical storytellers at your institution? What traits do they appear to have in common?

REFERENCES

Data Quality Campaign (2014a). *Empowering teachers with data: Policies and practices to promote educator data literacy.* Washington, DC.

Data Quality Campaign (2014b). *Teacher data literacy: It's about time.* Washington, DC.

Gartner, Inc. (2017). Gartner IT Glossary. Retrieved from www.gartner.com/it-glossary/self-service-analytics.

Honda, H., Knight, W., Kelly, H., Morimoto, Y., & Coughlin, M. A. (2017, June 1) Why do data and decisions often disagree? Paper presented at the Association for Institutional Research Annual Forum, Washington, DC.

Kim, Y. & Adler, M. (2015). Social scientists' data sharing behaviors: Investigating the roles of individual motivations, institutional pressures, and data repositories. *International Journal of Information Management, 35*(4): 408–418.

Kim, Y. & Zhang, P. (2015). Understanding data sharing behaviors of STEM researchers: The role of attitudes, norms, and data repositories. *Library & Information Science Research, 37*(3): 189–200.

Pienta, A., Alter, G., & Lyle, G. (2010). The enduring value of social science research: The use and reuse of primary research data. *Paper presented at The Organisation, Economics and Policy of Scientific Research.* Torino, Italy.

Swing. R. L. & Ross. L. E. (2016). A new vision for institutional research. In D. Paris (Ed.), *Change*, (pp. 6–13). Retrieved from www.airweb.org/Resources/IR Studies/Pages/A-New-Vision-for-Institutional-Research.aspx.

Terenzini, P. (1993). On the nature of institutional research and the knowledge and skills it requires. *Research in Higher Education, 34*(1): 1–10.

Tracy, S. (2016). *Why you should hire an empirical storyteller as your next data analyst.* Retrieved from www.sapientnitro.com/content/dam/sapientnitro/influence/insights/pdf/2016/SapientNitro_Insights_Empirical_Storyteller.pdf.

Chapter 12

Identifying and Mitigating Data Risk

Nancy D. Floyd and Yvonne Kirby

INTRODUCTION

The work of data functions within higher education is often compared to accounting. Data reporting, at its simplest, consists of toting up counts of students, courses and credit hours, degrees and awards, faculty and employees, averaging salaries, summing student grants and loans and institutional budget items. Those counts and summations, sliced and diced by all types of levels and modifiers, are then sent to entities that require or request them. Some entities are statutory or regulatory (e.g., the Integrated Postsecondary Education Data System or IPEDS), some entities publicly profile institutions (think college guidebooks like US News & World Report). Other entities serve as data exchanges where an institution submits data and in exchange, gains access to data from other institutions that are not available otherwise—included here are higher education consortia such as the American Association of Universities Data Exchange (AAUDE) and the Consortium for Student Retention Data Exchange (CSRDE). Often these same data are used within the institution to provide the basis for internal evaluation and decision-making, the cultivation of which is the primary focus of this volume.

What they have in common is the need for carefully documented and defined procedures, the use of standards that are often negotiated and defined in consultation with other institutions, and a foundation of empirical evidence. It is surprising then that some common concepts in accounting have not made their way into the language of data management in higher education. One such concept is that of risk, the assessment of risk in data management and planning for the mitigation of risk.

A business entity defines risk as any vulnerability that may threaten the ability to carry out or continue a planned course of action to maximize value to shareholders (Committee of Sponsoring Organizations: COSO, 2004). These vulnerabilities can be entirely of a company's own making, entirely external, or a combination of both. They can impact any level of the company's function, from the high level of the economic and political environment in which it operates, down to the low level of specific material availability and quality. These vulnerabilities can be extremely short-term risks, or very long-term risks. There can be known safeguards against risks, where there is some general idea of how to lessen or remove their impact, or no way whatsoever of predicting the impact of the risk. Risk appetite (COSO, 2004) is a means of defining and quantifying the level and type of risk that an entity is prepared to accept, and for which it will plan, as a cost of performing its function.

This chapter will briefly review the history of risk management as an area of study, including its theoretical inception and formalization, up to the very recent application of enterprise risk management (ERM) to the management of risk for colleges and universities. Some specific challenges faced by decision support leaders and professionals will be discussed in the context of managing and mitigating risk.

HISTORY OF ENTERPRISE RISK MANAGEMENT

Miller (1992) introduced the concept of centralizing risk management in an organization in an approach he called integrated risk management. The idea grew from a realization that even a modestly sized organization can find itself working at cross-purposes between departments or functions in attempting to address risk events, if the assessment and management of risk isn't centralized and regarded as a core function by upper management. Indeed, nearly a quarter of a century later, Rusert (2016) noted that only about half of executives gave their own organizations passing marks at being able to identify potential risks. Centralizing the identification, quantification, and management of risk is a core facet of ERM methodology.

The fledgling field was strengthened by the requirements for internal control and risk assessment in the Sarbanes-Oxley Act of 2002 (Pelletier, 2012). This led to early proliferation in industries heavily affected by risk, such as insurance, and became a focus of the internal audit function of business and industry. Currently, there is more than one accepted approach to ERM. The most commonly adopted framework was formalized by the Committee of Sponsoring Organizations (COSO) of the Treadway Commission in 2004. This document is known as the Framework; a major update to the Framework was proposed and was open to public comment through December 2016 (COSO, 2017).

Risk management made the jump to higher education via members of governing boards. In a 2009 report by United Educators and the Association of Governing Boards (AGB), ERM was defined as an approach that defines ownership of risk, attempts to quantify total cost, and urges the development of a culture where the evaluation and assessment of risk occurs at multiple levels of the organization. Early adopters of risk management in higher education included the University of Washington, the University of Texas, and Emory University (Pelletier, 2012).

Pelletier (2012) noted that risk is likely in four key functions of the enterprise: reporting, compliance, strategic, and operational risk. Typically, IR is managing at least part of the first two functions, and in optimal circumstances, involved in the last two.

SIMPLE INFORMATION RISKS

Let's discuss risks that may impact an institution with regard to two core functions: reporting and compliance. The most obvious risk to the reporting function is if reporting is being done badly or not at all. In either case, there is the possibility of the incurrence of fines, injuries to reputation from misreporting, various kinds of poor fit when other institutions attempt to benchmark metrics against your institution's data, and the risk of disseminating FERPA-protected data for purposes not authorized by students.

Fines

One of the most widely known types of risk that can occur in external reporting is that of fines; the National Center for Education Statistics (NCES) is mandated to collect data reported to the Integrated Postsecondary Education Data System (IPEDS) from institutions with a Program Participation Agreement (PPA) to award Title IV student financial aid. As part of this mandate, NCES partners with the Office of Federal Student Aid, who may assess fines against institutions for not reporting data in a timely and accurate manner. Even though it is a rare occurrence that an institution is assessed such fines, it behooves institutions to be aware of the timeline and requirements for statutory reporting and do everything possible to meet them.

Publishing Inaccurate Information

Another type of reporting risk is the publication or release of incorrect data, either inadvertently or deliberately. In the type of reporting error that occurs inadvertently, it can often go unnoticed and the data are used for summarizations that merely present an incorrect picture of activity at the institution. The potential impact can range from being large to insignificant. It is in an institution's best interests to establish routine systematic quality checks wherever data are externally reported. These can be comparing data against previous years' values or those of a group of close peers or comparators. This also helps to put information into context by identifying acceptable ranges and thresholds of values.

There are many acceptable strategies for mitigating the risk of mistakes that result in incorrect reporting. One common practice is to make sure that multiple analysts have reviewed or attempted to affirm all metrics that leave the office, prioritizing high-impact metrics such as those used in ranking formulas or by state legislatures. Whenever possible, it is helpful to attempt to validate counts using two different methodological approaches. If a single institution is generating metrics that are also being generated by a system office, it can be very illuminating to check those counts against each other.

Simply confirming that logic used in a query was appropriate and that alternative query approaches yield the same results may not be adequate; after all, this assumes the data being queried are accurate and that there are effective standardized operational definitions within the enterprise data warehouse.

The key to whatever system you put in place for data verification and validation is to be crystal clear about definitions being used to ensure that apples are being counted as apples, and to do it systematically. Open source queries and sharing of information is key. Also, be sure to design a set procedure for what occurs when a mistake is found—at what point in the reporting process will this generate an attempt to change the metric at its source, and under what circumstances will the analyst allow the metric to stand as it was reported? There are compelling arguments to be made for both approaches at different points in the reporting chain.

When incorrect reporting is not inadvertent but deliberate, the management of the institution needs to actively engage in weighing the value of the real or perceived advantage to be gained from such behavior with the accompanying cost of being discovered. Too often, such plans are made by too small a group of people within the institution to make this assessment. If ERM is in place, such conversations should involve the highest levels of the organization with the uppermost management explicitly owning this decision. If indeed it is strategy, upper management should be prepared to discuss and defend their decision to a variety of constituencies, including to their own governing boards before the decision is made. A comprehensive ERM strategy should include contingencies to ensure that a small number of employees cannot make such decisions without first informing stakeholders and upper management.

An interesting illustration is the case of Emory University, who was among the institutions cited by Pelletier (2012) as an exemplar of enterprise risk management, in the same year that they admitted inaccuracies in their reporting to US News & World Report, IPEDS, the Common Data Set, and other publications. To the institution's credit, they identified the issues and those responsible, making a full disclosure. They submitted corrected information for the current year, and prominently displayed a "Corrective Action Plan for Data Collection and Reporting" (Lewis, 2012) on their website, along with published FAQs. This document describes the implementation of a common "code book" whose content would be jointly determined and agreed upon by representatives of the functions involved in external reporting: admissions, the provost, and managed and owned by the director of institutional research.

US News & World Report maintains that the inaccuracies reported by Emory would not have changed their ranking score for the most recent two years for which inaccurate information was submitted (Morse, 2012). However, it is not possible for users to quantify whether or how such behavior would have changed the institutional reputation score, a metric that is accumulated from institutional reputation surveys sent to the chief officers of other institutions, who use their own perception of peer institutions to assign reputation scores. In the 2017 model, institutional reputation received a 22.5% weight, the largest single weight of any indicator in the model (Morse & Brooks, 2016). In this example, the risk lies in the possibility of longer lasting ranking-formula harm to an institution found to be gaming their metrics than the desired boost attained from the gaming.

A less obvious pitfall to an institution attempting to engage in such gaming is the need to make their information consistent to multiple reporting sources without creating a significant downside that impacts a different metric than the one they were trying to improve. For example, it is possible to use multiple operational definitions of whom the faculty are depending on which report or item is being completed or addressed. An institution choosing to use a very restrictive definition for who constitutes full-time instructional faculty with the intention of maximizing their average faculty salaries, as reported to AAUP and consequently used in the US News & World Report ranking formula, can find that they've inadvertently driven down their student–faculty ratio and their percentage of full-time faculty, also used in the US News & World Report ranking formula. So, it is considered a best practice to thoroughly investigate all of the possible interpretations of these metrics and work alongside management to develop a holistic approach that will tell the institution's best story, while not exposing the institution to accusations of cheating. Because the number of employees or case counts are published in each of these reports, such redefinition can be obvious.

A related caution: higher education managers should be careful when attaching, for example, US News & World Report rank position or the achievement of a certain benchmark to individual employees' performance evaluations or pay status. The responsibility for reaching an institutional metric should be planned, communicated, borne, and shared by all of the relevant stakeholders of the institution.

Poor Fit in Benchmarks

Higher education institutions of all sizes seek out and use data from their own institution as well as others to make strategic decisions or engage in performance-related comparisons. The universe of IPEDS data is made available through the NCES "Use the Data" portal (formerly the Data Center). State higher education data systems and independent institutional consortia share data with member institutions, as do a myriad of specialized data exchange groups. If institutions within these groups are using different definitions or are not striving to make their definitions clear so that members can judge comparability for themselves, then these comparisons can potentially lead to the wrong decisions. Making strategic decisions for the institution based on bad information is a very damaging potential risk.

Let's illustrate this problem using student residency. At most public institutions, there are different tuitions and charges for students who are attending from the state where the institution is located, with the justification being that since the student and/or their family have paid into the state's tax fund, some of that tax money found its way to support the institution and this is expressed in the offering of a lower tuition cost to people who have already borne part of that cost. Students who are attending from other states often have their own much higher tuition rate, and there may also be an in-between district level. On the student's behalf, residency may be established in a variety of ways, often involving the establishment of proof that the student or their family have paid state taxes for a certain period of time.

However, the field that establishes "residency" in the institutional enterprise data system can show verification to ensure that the student has a right to in-state tuition, or it might reflect the student's permanent or parent address, or it might reflect the state where they completed high school. Or, in the case of an international student, it might reflect the country of origin in their Student and Exchange Visitor Program (SEVIS) documentation. All of these possibilities may be used by institutions to respond to the breakdowns of students by residency in IPEDS, the Common Data Set, or other published datasets for comparison. And I am aware of only one—not a national resource—where a definition is specified or the respondent can indicate how residency is defined by their institution.

When institutions report data using their local, accepted-within-their-institution definition and do not research how others may be defining it or ignoring nationally-accepted/required definitions, it can result in faulty comparison data. For example, IPEDS does not ask for residency breakdown for "in-state" headcount, but this information, when combined with aid received by income level, is inextricably built into the net price calculation. Taking the example one step further, the US Department of Education's College Affordability and Transparency Center reviews the net price information reported to IPEDS and then lists the institutions with the highest net price or largest percentage increase in net price. When an institution is included in either one of these lists, whether it be due to bad information on who constitutes an in-state student or due to other circumstances at the institution, it can have an enormous impact on external institutional profile to potential incoming students. When the institution remains on the list for three consecutive years, additional reporting is required. It behooves institutions to follow the trail of not only how your institution is reporting but also how your likely peers and comparators are reporting as well.

Exposing Students to Privacy Risks

Because higher education professionals traffic in so much student data, they are typically as familiar with FERPA (the Family Educational Rights & Privacy Act) regulations as the employees of the records office or other campus guardian of FERPA. Data requests are typically subject to close scrutiny for a variety of FERPA risks, and so data professionals are adept at these discussions. The complex aggregation involved in much reporting is often used as the FERPA shield; we rely heavily on cell sizes greater than a small few to ensure that we aren't crossing the line of FERPA violation.

What can often escape our scrutiny is the subsequent downmarket use of unit record data that we provide to requestors or student unit record data that may be provided to a third party. Indeed, student unit record data are sometimes used in a way that potentially compromises their protected and fair use—this can also happen within the institution. The institution needs to have a clear picture of its responsibility and the extent to which it will protect individual students from having their information used in a way that the student them-selves did not sanction.

Most student privacy conversations center on FERPA and HIPAA (the Health Information Portability and Accountability Act of 1996), which applies even more stringent protective guidelines since it centers on sensitive patient information. Those conversations may even involve an institution's IRB (institu-tional review board) or other body that is tasked with ensuring that anyone involved in providing data for sponsored research has granted fully informed consent. But many institutions do not submit internal studies or institutional research to IRB. We may pass certain types of requests or language in a contract with a software or service provider to the institution's office of general counsel. But rarely does internally conducted student research, such as student success or retention research, include the step of asking how the research impacts the students on whom the research was collected and whether the institution is per-mitted to use their information in that way.

The burgeoning field of analytics in higher education has prompted reconsid-eration. Sclater and Bailey (2015) attempted to put together a "code of practice" to follow in determining the proper use of student data in what they called learning analytics. This would include a broad slate of interventions that are designed to improve student retention and success. Because they were writing from the UK perspective, their specific legal framework matched what was in place at that time in the European Union, but their core advice is universally applicable: inform students whenever possible of all the purposes that their data may be used for, allow them to opt out where possible, and document that they have been informed in situations where opting out is not possible. Above all else, potential risk to students must be minimized. Transparency is key. Institutions must assess their own internal uses of student data to see if such practices are being followed and the potential risk to the institution if they are not. Additionally, institutions must closely police contractual agreements with third-party vendors who receive unit record data to ensure that the data cannot be sold or used downmarket for purposes other than the one in the contract, and that a secure method of storage and data disposal is in place at all times.

COMPLEX DATA RISKS

Moving from risks inherent in reporting and compliance to those dealing with strategic goals and operations, the risk to the institution from having chronically unavailable or bad enterprise data is common and quite insidious. There is a universe of reasons as to why this may be the case at an institution; the impact of such a risk can be felt both within and outside the institution. Untangling the mess, as many higher education IR, IT, and academic affairs personnel are aware, can take an enormous amount of resources, and always occurs while the same inadequate data systems are being used to carry out necessary day-to-day operational functions. We can never just close up shop for a year to fix our data problems. The most practical approach is to use the principles of ERM to frankly assess the data quality situation at the institution, as well as its internal and external effects, and to begin to prioritize the most high-impact changes and controls to put into practice.

Many data professionals are devotees of the data dictionary or cookbook. A data dictionary is a document, sometimes maintained collectively as a Wiki, that spells out explicit definitions of how a variable in the data and/or reporting system is constructed. Good data dictionaries will attempt to do cradle-to-grave semantic documentation of how variables are related to each other, how they appear, are named, or what values they take from the point of input into the data system to the point of output when queried. Good, thorough data dictionaries are quite difficult to set up and are challenging to maintain.

Most data professionals who have had experience building a data dictionary know that the process typically raises more questions than it answers initially; frequently you need to first drill down into the detail to confirm what additional information feeds into the metric. How do data reflect the enterprise systems that created it? Are those enterprise systems themselves set up to portray the way that information is created and flows through the institution, or are the systems themselves limited by the software or system in which they're built? Are there functions of the institution that take precedence over other functions of the institution via the way their data lives in the enterprise systems? For example, academic departments are budgetarily obligated to use specified accounting codes that provide a picture of how money is flowing but these codes are often inadequate for showing academic activity or productivity. Is there so much inconsistency in the way the data systems are used by different units of the institution that the resulting data is at best confusing and at worst unusable? Are the data definitions in use so inflexible and stringent that the institution's procedures are set up to match the data definitions rather than the other way around? Are the data or crosswalks that make the data usable siloed off into one functional area? Are the data values so inconsistently maintained that longitudinal charts and graphs are of limited use?

During these conversations, it becomes apparent that some participating stakeholders have the ability to imagine new data systems or definitions that need to be created, while other stakeholders can only think about what already exists. Typically, both of these types of thinkers bring important and necessary skills to the data conversation, and it's crucial to have both types and all relevant functions at the table; however, appropriate people must be matched to appropriate assignments.

Another key area where the institution can experience intractable data system problems is the process of selecting and implementing enterprise or smaller-scale business intelligence (BI) software packages. Even well-planned ERP projects where a wide variety of data users and stakeholders are involved in the selection process can founder due to poor fit between the product and user expectations, or the lack of adequate preparation for staffing or training after implementation. This can create years-long delays in ramping up to the merely basic functionality of the system it replaced, let alone the planned-for comprehensive data system that was desired at the project's conception. Ideally, the chief institutional research officer (CIRO) should have a key position on the evaluation and selection team for such implementations if the system will interface with data that are intended for the "federated" data warehouse.

All of these are possible pitfalls that can interfere with the availability and appropriateness of data on which to base decisions, and yet all of them are avoidable. Traditionally, the function and practice of an IR office has been about providing answers to required questions, like the statutory reporting of IPEDS, however, IR offices are beginning to evolve into a function more like that of an enterprise institutional research—facilitating the answering of any question posed by anyone in the institution with a stake in the question. This is what is required if higher education is to fully embrace the concept of decision support in a data culture. Swing and Ross (2016) described the CIRO as being the center of a federated system of enterprise data that is interrelated by design so that the answer to any possible question becomes a reality.

So, if we think of the simple data risks of fines, misreporting, poor benchmarking, and data security violations as being the "known unknown" of enterprise risk, this more complex type of risk is the "unknown known"—what is it that we cannot measure because our data systems, tools, or definitions are inadequate to perform the task? What information is being masked by bad implementation and could it help us if we moved intentionally to measure it better?

This is where the IR function is a natural partner and the logical home to the concepts of shared data governance and the chief data officer. The IR function itself is typically one of the only places in the institution where all or most functional siloes come together: student data of several types, financial data, personnel data, facility and physical plant data, fundraising or advancement data, even library data. Because IR analysts often have skill in using many of these types of data, the IR office is a natural home for an approach that extends the data dictionary or cookbook into a true shared data governance system, fundamental for the federated system described by Swing and Ross (2016).

Kelly (2015) describes such an implementation of the chief data officer role at the University of South Carolina as a "federator" of enterprise data rather than a "governor." He describes a system of shared data governance that is managed and supervised by upper management data stewards, but that is set up and maintained by the data users themselves: "... those who best understand the data and bear the legal, regulatory, and compliance risks pertaining to it." This is consistent with the ERM perspective that the ability to assess risk lies—indeed, must lie—at multiple levels within the organization. It must be managed and prioritized centrally, but it must rely on eyes, ears, and brains at all responsibility levels to ensure identification of potential risks, implementation of mitigators, and feedback.

THE VANTAGE POINT: POSITIONING OF THE IR FUNCTION AND RISK ASSESSMENT

The position of the IR director and function within the management of the institution can have a significant impact on how effective that position can be in assessing both simple and complex data risks. Does the IR director spend their time primarily in data assembly, management and calculation, or have they been leveraged to deal directly with functional areas to plan and execute reporting as an enterprise data expert? Are they sufficiently experienced, both in the industry and in the institution, to have the body of knowledge required to analyze data practices with an eye toward maximizing potential? Professionals who are involved heavily in the day-to-day bean counting and repetitive tasks may not have the bandwidth required to become a true CIRO. Institutions need to provide their IR directors with the time and supportive resources needed to develop these skills, if this is the desired outcome.

Vantage can also be affected by the institutional area that supervises the IR function and by how far down in the organizational chart the IR director is located. The types of projects assigned to IR directors who answer directly to a president, chancellor, or Board can be materially different from those assigned to IR directors who answer to a provost or dean of academic affairs. Those who answer to financial or IT units can be even further removed or have a very specific take on how data is used by the institution. Additionally, an IR director who is more than two levels removed from a chief executive of the institution may be too far down in the organization to be seen as an authoritative voice on data governance.

PRACTICAL SUGGESTIONS AND GUIDANCE: GETTING STARTED

We've covered a lot of areas of potential risk, made suggestions for possible mitigators, and asked many important questions for managers and stakeholders. The next question for readers of this chapter is: "How do I get started?". Tackling such a project for an institution of higher education, much as for a corporation or business entity, can take many forms. There is the COSO cube (Tufano, 2011) and a number of other organizing matrices or schemes for the conversation, all geared toward a slightly different intended audience. Since the discussion of risk and what to do about it is already very complex, the structure in which the discussion happens is best made simple. It should include:

- *Be proactive.* Often the risk conversation only starts after an adverse event has already happened; whereas this is the exact situation that ERM is intended to avoid, it can have a clarifying effect. Ideally, your institution is starting the risk conversation motivated by the desire to avoid such a situation.
- *Identify a champion.* Because the risk conversation is a complex one and can be made difficult by employees' natural hesitancy to speak frankly about processes at their workplaces that may not be optimal, it should have at least one high-placed, prominent champion who continually reinforces the importance of having an atmosphere in which conversations can be frank and the overarching goal of protecting the institution's function through ERM.
- *Understand organizational depth.* Pelletier (2012) urged involvement of employees and stakeholders at all levels of the organization to adequately assess risks. Whereas much of the literature on ERM, particularly for higher education, is written for audiences of board members and upper management, actual risk assessment needs to be done by those who are closest to the risk arena. So be sure to cut into the organization when assembling risk teams.
- *Create a risk assessment schedule.* Tufano (2011) cited a finding from the UE/AGB survey where more than half of respondents indicated that their organization was engaging in the identification of potential risks on an as-needed basis instead of on a regular cycle. Whereas there are some true "black swan" events for which no entity could adequately plan, the majority of risk events that happen in higher education are known possibilities that can be periodically

assessed and have quantifiable plans of action. It may make sense to incorporate risk assessment into three-year or five-year strategic plan cycles, and to revisit the subject quarterly or monthly to quickly assess the accuracy of guesses at risk.

■ *Prioritize data risks.* All of the matrix or cube schemes used to describe potential risks have as an organizing principle some version of a continuum of "could continue to function" to "will cease institutional functioning." Even simple risk assessment for a single office or function can be done with classification schemes that quantify disruption to normal operation. That disruption can be expressed on a wide variety of levels.

SUMMARY

This chapter defines and contextualizes risk management for application in higher education data management and reporting. Topics to be addressed include simple information risks such as the incurrence of fines, publication of inaccurate information, use of ill-fitting benchmarking data, and ensuring the appropriate use of student and staff data. More complex information risks include unassessed inadequacy of enterprise systems to allow for consistent use of information for decision support, lack of an adequate data governance structure, and lack of correct positioning of the institutional research staff to maximize efficacy.

DISCUSSION QUESTIONS

1. What safeguards are you currently using to ensure accurate reporting? How might you evaluate the efficacy of these methods?

2. Identify personnel (by name or role) in your institution now who should be assigned to a risk assessment team.

3. What are your current policies about ensuring the privacy of student or staff data? Do you have procedures in place to require data outsourcers to destroy data at the end of its useful life? Are these procedures pushed into required contractual agreements?

4. What is the profile of your chief institutional research officer? Do they have sufficient vantage at your institution to be leveraged to identify and safeguard against risks?

5. What types of risks challenge the performance of your unit now? Can you identify three or four aspects of these risks that would allow you to assess them?

REFERENCES

Committee of Sponsoring Organizations of the Treadway Commission. (2004). Enterprise risk management-integrated framework. [Press Release] Retrieved from www.coso.org/documents/Framework%20Reference%20Secured.pdf.

Committee of Sponsoring Organizations of the Treadway Commission. (2017). *COSO evaluating public comments on ERM update.* [Press Release] Retrieved from www.coso.org/Documents/News-COSO-ERM-Update-2017.pdf.

Kelly, M. (2015, June 8). The chief data officer in higher education. *Educause Review.* Retrieved from http://er.educause.edu/articles/2015/6/the-chief-data-officer-in-higher-education.

Lewis, E. (2012). *Corrective* action plan for data collection and reporting. [Press Release] Retrieved from http://news.emory.edu/special/data_review/action_plan.html.

Miller, K. D. (1992). A framework for integrated risk management in international business. *Journal of International Business Studies, 23*(2): 311–331.

Morse, R. (2012, August 17). Emory University misreported admissions data. [Blog post]. *US News.* Retrieved from www.usnews.com/education/blogs/college-rankings-blog/2012/08/17/emory-university-misreported-admissions-data.

Morse, R. and Brooks, E. (2016, September 12). Best colleges ranking criteria and weights. *US News.* Retrieved from www.usnews.com/education/best-colleges/articles/ranking-criteria-and-weights.

Pelletier, S. (2012). New strategies for managing risks: A balancing act for boards. *Trusteeship, 20*(1): 14–19.

Rusert, B. (2016). Guarding the company's good name. *Corporate Responsibility Magazine, 7*(3). Retrieved from www.thecro.com/vol-7-no-3-mayjune-2016/guarding-the-companys-good-name/.

Sclater, N. and Bailey, P. (2015). Code of practice for learning analytics. *Jisc.* Retrieved from www.jisc.ac.uk/guides/code-of-practice-for-learning-analytics.

Swing, R. L. & Ross, L. E. (2016). A new vision for institutional research. *Change: The Magazine of Higher Learning, 48*(2): 6–13.

Tufano, P. (2011). Managing risk in higher education. *Forum for the Future of Higher Education.* Retrieved from https://net.educause.edu/ir/library/pdf/ff1109s.pdf.

United Educators and the Association of Governing Boards of Universities and Colleges (2009). *The state of enterprise risk management at colleges and universities today.* Retrieved from http://agb.org/sites/agb.org/files/u3/AGBUE_FINAL.pdf.

Part IV

Putting the Culture Pieces Together

Chapter 13

Implementing the Data Culture

Kristina Powers and Angela E. Henderson

INTRODUCTION

Cultivating any type of a data culture in higher education is not easy. Creating an effective one is even more challenging. Thus, the purpose of this book has been to provide strategies for understanding the current data culture and identifying ways to make improvements. Time and reliable information are highly correlated and desirable by administrators. We could all use some extra time—no matter what the task is (e.g., presentation for the board or president, accreditation report, time to recruit new students, etc.). When we feel pressed for time, there may not have been sufficient effort devoted to reviewing, researching, or discussing a decision. With enough time to think—really think—you can have flashes of brilliance. But who has time to think? Perhaps to help accelerate those flashes of brilliance, consider this list of Practical Suggestions, compiled from the chapters in this book, to prompt your thinking.

We recognize that readers will be at different stages in cultivating process and that administrators do not have much time to develop creative ways to solve old problems. Having this backdrop in mind, this chapter has two goals: serve as a compendium of the sage advice provided in the Practical Suggestions portion of each chapter; and identify potential next steps of where you might go from here.

WAYS TO USE THE COMPENDIUM OF PRACTICAL SUGGESTIONS

Throughout each chapter, the author(s) provided Practical Suggestions. Those suggestions have been compiled into one list in Table 13.1. However, rather than the items reading like a disorganized grocery list, the suggestions are organized by three common challenges that administrators have when turning to resources for ideas: people, strategic planning, and resources and tools. The list

Table 13.1 Compendium of Practical Suggestions and Guidance

Category/Practical Suggestions	Chapter										
	1	2	3	4	5	7	8	9	10	11	12
People											
Designate a change agent to shepherd organizational change	X										
Emphasize the benefits and advantages to be gained from data-informed decisions	X										
Encourage employee use of data		X									
Engage with employees on the possibilities of data		X									
Educate employees on how to manipulate and use data		X									
Start with a lunch		X									
Review executive sponsor concerns		X									
Gain insight into organizational culture		X									
Understand the campus data culture		X									
Hold a data summit		X									
Build relationships within the environment and be present in that environment			X								
Blend out of the current leadership circle and department/division to obtain context from other units			X								
Move through multiple circles to conduct some preliminary research			X								
Identify individuals for a committee who can look holistically at the institution			X								
Engage with new people entering the institution (or committee)			X								
Appoint an institutional context officer			X								
Hire for data competency				X							
Evaluate and reward data use				X							
Uncover potentially unconscious inclinations, ideas, or feelings about words and the ways they contribute to understanding an individual's thinking about data					X						

Category/Practical Suggestions

Category/Practical Suggestions	Chapter											
	1	2	3	4	5	6	7	8	9	10	11	12
Reconsider questions in light of possible cognitive bias					X							
Invest in signature relationship practices						X						
Ensure the requisite skills						X						
Understand role clarity and task ambiguity						X						
Engage the Board							X					
Involve the entire college							X					
Infuse data into the relationship							X					
Connect with state and federal colleagues							X					
Lead the initiative							X					
Build relationships with key people in various areas								X				
Identify the "purple people" in your university								X				
Try to understand other people's perspectives								X				
Create a group of "Power Data Providers"								X				
Create a "Who's Who Data Directory"								X				
Commit to not shopping around								X				
Discuss the data									X			
Understand cultural changes do not happen overnight											X	
Strategic Planning												
Conduct a data culture audit	X											
Ensure broad awareness and shared understanding of key metrics	X											
Consider a data maturity audit		X										
Review old IT project charters and whitepapers		X										
Examine peer campuses		X										
Conduct a review of data policies and procedures		X										
Select terms for initiatives which are positive and promote trust			X									

continued

Table 13.1 Continued

Category/Practical Suggestions	Chapter											
	1	2	3	4	5	6	7	8	9	10	11	12
Benchmark against other institutions, display trends over time, and examine group differences to gain additional context			X									
Including data as part of regular meeting agendas				X								
Be open to new ideas					X							
Create an organizational culture adapted to data						X						
Prevent initiative fatigue							X					
Create a culture of data integrity								X				
Consider the big picture									X			
Become a storyteller											X	
Identify a champion												X
Resources and Tools												
Make data usable	X											
Take a course in storytelling		X										
Join one or more of the numerous higher education professional networks			X									
Read and learn about the history of the institution			X									
Speed dating through data				X								
Show & Tell				X								
Communicate key data				X								
Create data dashboards				X								
Host a "Data Day"				X								
Constantly review processes and procedures							X					
Prioritize professional development							X					
Publicize what is already known and available								X				
Establish processes and share them								X				
Practice patience and persistence								X				

Category/Practical Suggestions	Chapter											
	1	2	3	4	5	6	7	8	9	10	11	12
Develop documentation									X			
Anticipate follow-up questions										X		
Avoid data overload										X		
Ensure data tell a complete story										X		
Promote clarity										X		
Create strategic data visualizations										X		
Use your campus mythology										X		
Embrace branding										X		
Become a storyteller											X	
Be proactive												X
Understand organizational depth												X
Identify a champion												X
Create a risk assessment schedule												X
Prioritize data risks												X

is intended to help problem-solve or to generate possible solutions to data culture challenges. These three topics also parallel accreditation criteria and standards, which many administrators consider regularly.

Certainly, you can use the list by reading it from top to bottom; it may be a good idea to scan through it. The list includes the chapter where the suggestion can be found so that if you see one or more suggestions that are appealing, you are can turn to the corresponding chapter to read more details. The list is organized into categories or problems that you, as a current or aspiring administrator may encounter or wish to address. Once you've selected a category that is of interest, read through the suggestions and consider how it can be applied toward improving your issue. The list can help generate some ideas; it is not implementary but the chapters contain more details.

SUMMARY

We hope this book, as well as this chapter, have been helpful in advancing your ability to cultivate a data culture. Since most institutions' data cultures have developed organically, or with minimal shaping, many administrators are finding that intentional interventions to cultivate a data culture has potential to yield institutional efficiencies as well as new ideas. While data collection and analysis have been in place for decades, we believe that the next phase includes better use of the people, resources, and strategic planning to cultivate a data culture.

Biographies

EDITORS

Kristina Powers, PhD is President of K Powers Consulting Inc., a national IPEDS trainer, a Research Fellow on Student Achievement with the WASC Senior College and University Commission and Vice President of Institutional Effectiveness & Planning at Patten University. Previously she served as Associate Vice President of Institutional Research Services at Bridgepoint Education, the parent company of Ashford University (San Diego), was Assistant to the President for Strategic Research & Analysis at Valdosta State University (Georgia) where she served as the head of institutional research, and the 2016 President of the California Association for Institutional Research (CAIR). Other higher education roles have included, lead author for the Statements of Aspirational Practice for Institutional Research with the Association for Institutional Research (AIR), teaching and developing institutional research and higher education administration courses at four institutions, conducting policy education research at the Florida Legislature, consulting services at MGT of America, and an admissions advisor at the State University of New York, College at Brockport. She earned her doctorate from Florida State University in Educational Leadership and Policy Studies with a concentration in Higher Education Policy and a Master's in Higher Education Administration from Florida State University, and a Bachelor's from the State University of New York, College at Brockport. She publishes and presents in the areas of higher education administration and organization, institutional research, as well as student success with a focus on retention and graduation rates using national databases and institutional data. Her recent co-edited book, *Organization and Administration in Higher Education*, published by Routledge, released the second edition in March

2017. She has served as issue co-editor and author for *New Directions of Institutional Research*.

Angela E. Henderson, PhD serves as Director of Institutional Research & Effectiveness at Stetson University, where she is responsible for development and dissemination of institutional data reports and analytics. Henderson's areas of expertise and interest include data-informed analyses, data visualization, and integration of data to guide institutional decision-making processes. Throughout her fifteen years of higher education experience, she has presented numerous sessions on these topics at national and regional conferences including the Association for Institutional Research, the Southern Association of Colleges and Schools, the American Educational Research Association, and EDUCAUSE. Henderson has also served as issue co-editor and author for *New Directions of Institutional Research*. She received an MA in English from Georgia Southern University, an MLIS from Valdosta State University, and a PhD in Education and Human Resource Studies from Colorado State University.

AUTHORS

Eric S. Atchison is the Director of System Analysis, Research & Enrollment Management for the Mississippi Institutions of Higher Learning (IHL) and is the Principal of The Atchison Research Collaborative, LLC (ARC). Atchison's responsibilities include overseeing statistical analysis, admissions, and remedial policies for the eight public universities within the IHL system, as well as serving as the IPEDS State Coordinator. His work involves continuous discussions about system-wide initiatives and data collection efforts to inform policies and programs. Through the ARC, Atchison provides analysis and training for a wide scope of projects with partners from postsecondary institutions, research organizations, and non-profit agencies. He has also served as a member of the faculty at Delta State University and Mississippi Gulf Coast Community College.

Karinda Rankin Barrett, PhD serves as the Associate Vice-Chancellor for Academic and Student Affairs at the Division of Florida Colleges where she focuses on policy related to academic program development, articulation, distance learning developmental education, and supporting underserved students. Prior to her work at the Division, she was the founding director of the Center for Professional Enrichment at Tallahassee Community College. She also worked at Florida State University as the Associate Director of the Hardee Center for Women in Higher Education, as well as in student affairs positions at Western Carolina University and the University of South Carolina.

Michael M. Black, EdD serves as Director of Institutional Effectiveness at Valdosta State University (Valdosta, GA), where he attended as an undergraduate and graduate student. He earned a Doctor of Education in Higher Education from the Florida State University and has worked full time in public higher education for sixteen years in areas such as finance, policy administration, institutional research, strategic planning, assessment, compliance, accreditation, program review, and academic planning. He reads and writes about higher education history and has completed two books about Valdosta State University's history along with several other books related to his family history.

P. Daniel Chen, PhD is an Associate Professor of Higher Education in the Department of Counseling and Higher Education at the University of North Texas. Prior to becoming a faculty member, he was a research analyst with the National Survey of Student Engagement (NSSE). Chen has many years of experience conducting survey design, psychometric analysis, and quantitative research. Chen's research focuses on student success, assessment of student outcomes, institutional effectiveness, STEM education, and spirituality in higher education. His research has been published in the *Journal of Higher Education* and *Research in Higher Education*, among others.

Ah Ra Cho, PhD is an Assistant Professor and Director of Assessment and Evaluation at the Michigan State University College of Osteopathic Medicine. She received her PhD in Higher Education from the University of North Texas, Masters in Higher Education and Student Affairs from Baylor University, and Bachelors of Arts in Biology from Texas A&M University.

Stephanie Douglas, PhD currently serves as the Assistant Dean for the College of Business and Economics at the University of Wisconsin—Whitewater. Her areas of expertise include organizational change, organizational behavior, leadership, gender differences in consumer behavior, higher education marketing, and online education. She earned her PhD in Education and Human Resource Studies from Colorado State University. She is active in accreditation reviews for the Association to Advance Collegiate Schools of Business (AACSB), as well as serving on committees for Wisconsin Women in Higher Education Leadership (WWHEL). Her research and teaching are in the areas of social entrepreneurship, organizational behavior, organizational change theory, leadership development, and market research.

Nancy D. Floyd, PhD is the Director of Institutional Analytics at North Carolina State University. In this role, she coordinates the nightly upload and edit of enterprise data to a state system data mart, as well as the conversion of this data to reporting tools for the University community, and serves as an IPEDS Keyholder. She and her team have been working to convert the

183

office's legacy static reporting to a dynamic platform using SAS Visual Analytics and coax the institution toward shared data governance.

Eric Godin serves as Associate Vice-Chancellor for Research & Analytics at the Division of Florida Colleges. In this role, he oversees data requests, analysis, and reports related to Florida's twenty-eight state colleges. His goal for the Research & Analytics team at the Division is to increase the use and understanding of data from Florida's community college system to allow data-informed decision-making to promote student readiness, access, and success. Before joining the Division, Godin spent eight years working for two national higher education organizations, the Association for Institutional Research (AIR) and the Council of Independent Colleges (CIC).

Resche D. Hines, PhD is currently the Assistant Vice-President for Institutional Research and Effectiveness at Stetson University. Prior to joining Stetson, Dr. Hines served as the Assistant Vice-President for Enrollment Management and Director of Institutional Research at Chicago State University. Dr. Hines is a results driven, focused, and effectual leader with the proven ability to provide enhanced organizational leadership through data-informed decision-making in academic affairs, strategic planning, enrollment measurement and institutional change management in Higher Education and not for profit sectors.

Wendy Kallina, PhD is Director of Academic Analytics at Kennesaw State University and a member of the Complete College Georgia state team. Dr. Kallina has presented at conferences including the Southern Association for Institutional Research (SAIR), the Association for Institutional Research (AIR), the Southern Association of Colleges and Schools Commission on Colleges (SACSCOC), and the Society for College and University Planning (SCUP). Her presentation and workshop topics include data collection and forensics, beginning and advanced statistical analysis, forecasting, predictive analytics, assessment, information reporting and presentation, institutional culture and planning, and strategies and metrics for student success.

Yvonne Kirby serves as the Director of Institutional Research & Assessment at Central Connecticut State University. She coordinates the office's federal, state, and mandatory reporting as well as coordinating campus-wide assessment activities. Kirby's experience with data and institutional effectiveness has contributed to her membership in serving on the re-accreditation steering committees for two different universities as they prepare(d) their ten-year self-studies. She has served as an IPEDS Keyholder and is a long-time user of national databases for benchmarking at the state, regional, and national level to help inform senior leadership in support of institutional policy decisions and long-range planning.

Paula S. Krist, PhD has been a consultant to many institutions of higher education, domestic and international. She is regularly invited to present at academic and professional conferences. She is active with the California Association for Institutional Research. At the University of San Diego, she is a member of the President's Cabinet, the University Assessment Committee, the Strategic Planning Support Committee, and the WSCUC steering committee. She regularly serves on accreditation review committees and advises PhD candidates. She works with both academic and student affairs, helping faculty and student support personnel to conduct assessments, as well as analyzing data and interpreting results.

Jeffrey L. Pellegrino, PhD, MPH serves as Professor/Program Director of Foundational Education & Health Professions at Aultman College of Nursing & Health Science and has previously held positions in Strategic Initiatives/Quality Improvement along with faculty professional development where he supported individual through university initiatives. Currently, his scholarship includes building evidence based first aid education practices. He serves as the editor-in-chief of the *International Journal of First Aid Education*.

Jason F. Simon, PhD is the Assistant Vice-President—Data, Analytics, and Institutional Research at the University of North Texas. Jason also serves as an affiliate faculty member in Higher Education. He leads a comprehensive enterprise-wide data warehouse program designed to bring together data sources across enrollment management, finance, academic affairs, and student affairs to promote data-informed decision-making. Over his twenty-two-year career, Jason has lead teams in advancement, student affairs, academic affairs, and finance and administration. He brings these diverse perspectives to his work in supporting creative data solutions for strategically important challenges facing his institution.

Mihaela Tanasescu MD, ScD is a Provost at Trident University International. She previously served as the Executive Dean of the College of Health, Human Services and Science and the Acting Vice-President for Academic Affairs at Ashford University. Mihaela has published peer-reviewed research and has served on WSCUC review teams. She received her Doctor of Science from the Harvard School of Public Health, her MS from the University of Connecticut, and her MD from the Carol Davila University of Medicine and Pharmacy in Romania.

Elna van Heerden, DEd serves as the Associate Vice-President, Institutional Effectiveness and New Programs at Trident University International. She is an experienced Higher Education Executive, whose career spans over twenty-four years. During this time, she has served as Chief Academic Officer, founding Dean, Vice-President of Assessment and Academic

Quality, Director of Assessment and Faculty. Her areas of expertise are institutional effectiveness, assessment, academic quality assurance, and online education. Elna earned her doctoral degree in Philosophy of Education from the University of South Africa. She is a graduate of the first class of WASC's Assessment Leadership Academy, has been appointed for a three-year term to the WSCUC Interim Review Committee since January 2015, and serves on WSCUC visiting teams.

Lori Williams, PhD serves as WSCUC Vice-President, responsible for strategic initiatives and policy issues, and as liaison to a portfolio of WSCUC institutions. Previously, she was Provost and Chief Academic Officer at Ashford University, Vice-Provost of Curriculum Development and Innovation at Kaplan University, Vice-President of Product Strategy and Development at Laureate Education, Executive Director of the Center for Student Success at Walden University, and held administrative roles at Saint Michael's College and Middlebury College. Lori has taught extensively, as professor, thesis advisor, and mentor. She enjoys time outdoors hiking with her husband and dog, gardening, yoga, and movies.

Index

121, 128–129, 136–137, 151–152, 166–167; academic 52, 70; complex 70; designated 146; for determining appropriate data sources 114, 123; developmental 66; educational 81, 91; four-part 66; reporting 162; selection 167; systematic 118; tenure-track 132; two-part 119

professional development 44, 50, 73, 76, 90, 178; activities 20; job-embedded 73; offerings 76; and support 76

professional expertise 85–86, 88, 91

professional learning communities 73

professional networks 37, 88, 178

professionals 29, 85, 91–92, 148–149, 160, 168; higher educational 148; line-of-business 147

program management, outsourced 61

Program Participation Agreement 161

programs 13, 47, 49, 59–60, 69, 72, 84, 87, 90, 92, 113, 129, 133–134, 154; attendance 117; cohesive 84; completers 117; degree 48; existing 59; federal financial aid 60; five-year review 154; grant 92; improvement 32; institutionalized reward 51; prioritization 79

projects 14, 38, 51, 71, 88–90, 92–93, 104, 150, 168–169; data 13; department's 93; new 90; recorded oral history 38; service-learning 88; successful 151; well-planned ERP 167

promotion records 100

prospective students 5–6, 131, 133–135

protocols 107, 117, 119; for external reporting 100; review research 119

providers 7, 58, 60, 66, 106–107, 132, 177; service 60, 66, 165; third-party 58

PTAC *see* Privacy Technical Assistance Center

quality 43, 47–48, 62, 73, 80, 89, 118, 120–121, 154, 160; assurance processes 49; data 60; systematic 161

questions 57, 59, 61–62, 64–66, 74, 98–99, 101–107, 118–119, 126–132, 136, 138–139, 149–151, 154–155, 166–167; and answers 43, 61, 113, 118; common 102, 134; complex 129–130; critical 137; explicit 62; framing of 43, 75; important 169; institutional 102; interview 149; multiple 127; sample 7, 19, 35; underlying 150; varied 129

race 60, 115, 118; categories 118; and ethnicity 118, 121; reclassifying 121

RACI *see* Responsible, Accountable, Consulted, or Informed exercise

rates 63, 104, 129, 144; average DFW 144; graduation/retention 115; higher tuition 164; innovation's 47; institutional 135; job placement 59

raw data 8, 146

reforms 32, 85; comprehensive 84; initiatives 84

relationships 4, 18, 36, 44, 84–92, 104, 106, 122, 176–177; benefitting from honesty 87, 92; building of 9, 80, 84–85, 87, 89–91, 93, 104, 106; data-based 90; of senior leaders 90; significant 81; strategic 75

reports 6–8, 32–36, 51, 53, 58–60, 62, 66, 103–106, 113, 126–131, 133–136, 138–140, 143–147, 163; accreditation 175; for administrators 105; for college departments 90; continuous improvement of 53; customized grade distribution 75, 144; and data structures 121–122, 126–130, 133; enrollment 113; requirements 117, 143

research 28, 30, 52, 63, 77–78, 98, 142, 144, 155, 164–165; conducting competitor 59; discipline-based educational 51; internal 101; scientific 47; sponsored 60, 165; student 165; units 85